New
Specially Selected
Jokes and Stories
for All Occasions

by
Al Schock

Melvin Powers
Wilshire Book Company

12015 Sherman Road, No. Hollywood, CA 91605

ACKNOWLEDGEMENTS

To all the members of my family—my wife Phyllis, my sons Bernie, Paul and Steve, daughters Bobbie and Barb, their spouses and also to my three grandsons (Bernie & Cathy's boys) Nathan, Andrew and Jered. Jered, a first year straight A high school student, did an especially good job in correcting punctuation mistakes and for his recommendations on the choice of some words. I thank them all for their willingness to serve as guinea pigs and test targets for the material contained herein and especially for their tolerance and understanding.

To Lynne Steele who wore multiple secretarial hats serving the Lieutenant Governor of the state of South Dakota, my son and his financial services business, and then on occasion when time permitted to do the typing for this book.

To Kim Pekas who helped organize and type the final draft of this book.

To the thousands of people who have heard me tell many of the stories within these covers and a special thanks to the hundreds of emcees and speakers, many now forgotten, who directly or indirectly were contributors of much of the material in this book.

Finally to my wonderful sister-in-law, Lucille Mannes, who recently died of cancer who handed me this quatrain after one of my emceeing performances.

If he can remember so many stories
And all the details that mold them,
Why can't he recall with equal skill
How many times he's told them?

A GOOD LEADER

IS A PERSON

WHO SOLVES

MORE PROBLEMS

THAN HE

CREATES

ABOUT THE AUTHOR

Al Schock is an achiever. It will come as no surprise to his many friends that he's been writing books. Having spoken or emceed more than 3,000 functions, he has written a much needed book on emceeing (and unrelated items based on his own experiences). Al believes that too many of our meetings, conventions and banquets are poorly planned, hum drum, nonproductive and just plain boring.

This compilation of stories, jokes, anecdotes, one liners and puns with some good sage wisdom thrown in is typical of Al. When Al has something good going for him, he wants to share it with his fellow man. As a matter of fact he frequently insists on it.

A veteran of World War II, holder of the bronze star and purple heart, he came out of Army hospitals to get a masters degree at the University of Wisconsin. After a two-year stint as professor at South Dakota State University, he and his brother, Ozzie, started a dairy operation with $500 of operating capital and a pile of bank loan rejection slips. When the Schock brothers sold their dairy enterprise to Land-O-Lakes in 1968, they had 400 employees and 52 branches covering an area including five states.

In 1959, the brothers started a second company named *Nordica International* that produced cultures for the manufacturer of all types of cultured dairy products. They licensed the processing procedures internationally. They always insisted that all of the employees be share holders. When the culture company was sold to a French company, Rhone Poulenc, in 1989, the French company paid the shareholders more money than was paid by the U.S. for the Louisiana purchase in 1803 which included South Dakota.

Al is a national, state and community leader who has travelled worldwide. Among his accomplishments are the following:

— Served as first United Fund Chairman of Sioux Falls.
— Served four years as president of the Sioux Falls Development Foundation. During his reign, land was purchased and developed bringing dozens of firms to his community creating thousands of new jobs that led in part to Sioux Falls being named by *Money Magazine* as the most livable city in the United States in 1993.
— Served as chairman of the Board of Governors of Lions International, the world's largest service club.
— Served twelve years on the Board of Regents of Augustana College.
— Received an honorary doctorate degree in science from South Dakota State University.
— Was candidate for U.S. Senate.
— Received the South Dakota Press Association's distinguished service award.
— Served ten years as civilian aide to the Secretary of the Army for South Dakota and received the Department of the Army's highest distinguished service medal.
— Received the Sioux Falls Development Foundation's first "Spirit of Sioux Falls Award."

Al is author of several books including *Brothers in War* and *Words of Wisdom for Children and Grandchildren.*

Darlene Gage, Al's former secretary states, "Al is a gentle man with a keen wit and lively sense of humor. This anthology of some of his favorites, in addition to being enjoyable reading, will provide emcees and speakers a ready source of useful material to enliven their presentations."

PREFACE

Go to any bookstore where you find books sectionalized by subject matter and content, and you'll find few books dealing in stories, jokes, puns and anecdotes that can be read for pure enjoyment or used by emcees and public speakers.

In some bookstores in the humor section I have found books so raunchy in content that I would have been embarrassed to have anyone see me purchasing a copy.

In one of our early business ventures, my brother Ozzie and I employed over 400 people. Some were hired for their special skills and talents, but most of them could have been categorized as average workers. Many of these average workers moved into positions of greater responsibility and remuneration and often so because they possessed a superior sense of humor, knew how to tell a story that would evoke laughter among their fellow employees and add to the over all cheerfulness of the working place.

Some years ago someone handed me a promotional folder put out by a firm called *The Humor Project of Saratoga Springs, New York.* Two things caught my attention. One was a quote from George Burns who said "You can't help getting older, but you sure can help getting old." When in his 90's and recovering from brain surgery he stated that he would keep his appointment in Las Vegas plus some additional performances in other parts of the country. Asked why he was still performing at such a late age he said "Well, I've got to earn some money to put away for my retirement."

The other item that caught my attention stated that "Laughter is the shortest distance between two people. Humor is an effective way and a fun way to reach out and touch someone, to boost morale at work, to communicate serious messages with a light touch, all may make the world go round but laughter keeps us from getting dizzy. To increase your face value — smile."

In my book on *Emceeing and Public Speaking* (a few copies of the hard cover book are still available from the author), I devoted an entire chapter to the use of quips, puns, jokes and anecdotes and humorous poetry. Most especially the four-liner quatrain type. You will find a good number of these in this book. In this book I've also reprinted the entire section on the *ABC's of Telling and Remembering Stories.* By applying those guidelines you'll be amazed at how many stories, jokes and puns you will be able to recall and put to good use when the occasion calls for it.

It would take several volumes to list the hundreds of stories and quips that I've collected, written or embellished during my lifetime. The ones selected for this book should be usable with some adaptation for a long period of time.

There are few events that cannot benefit by the interjection of a bit of frivolity or a light touch of humor. Humor like music is almost universally appreciated. Most people with some training can tell stories and use humor with good effect for almost any occasion. For people who perform the function of emcee or moderator or chairperson, it is important to remember to keep things moving and to delight the audience when the occasion calls for it with your own wit and humor spiced with puns and stories that have been specifically selected for the occasion.

TABLE OF CONTENTS

THE ABC's OF
TELLING AND
REMEMBERING STORIES

The following list will serve as a guideline for things you should remember when using puns and telling anecdotes and stories:

A. Select material suitable for the occasion.
B. Memorize it thoroughly.
C. Avoid telling the audience, "And that reminds me..."
D. Never interrupt yourself while telling a story by saying, "Please stop me if you've heard this one before." Make the assumption, even when telling an old story, that this is the first time the audience has ever heard it. There are many old quips, anecdotes and stories that can be told in your own style and enjoyed by your audience, just as old songs are often resung and enjoyed, for instance, "My Wild Irish Rose" and "Let Me Call You Sweetheart."
E. If you find it necessary to use someone in the audience as a target for your quip or story, select that person carefully. Unless you know the person, and the story fits and has some degree of validity, using the wrong person will make you appear amateurish and your pun highly artificial. A much better practice is to use yourself in the style of a Jack Benny or Bob Hope — "You wouldn't believe what happened to me on the way here tonight . . .", or "A funny thing happened on the way to my office this morning."
F. Make certain that the anecdotes and stories that you select fit in and are relevant, smoothly connecting even disconnected parts of your presentation as you shift gears.
G. Avoid using stories that are too involved and too long.

H. Never forget the punch line.

I. Avoid the off-color or otherwise offensive story.

J. Use associations to help you remember puns, short stories and anecdotes. Notice that in the table of contents I have used major headings to provide name associations to help you retain and recall a vast number of stories and other appropriate material. In addition to using major headings, I also suggest that you make other associations for the stories and material that you want to remember on a more or less permanent basis.

For example, let us use a story given in this book under the heading of "Advice." The story is attributed to Frank Lloyd Wright, the famous architect. Though listing the story under "Advice" I could have also classified it under architects or builders. Few of us have a photographic mind or otherwise possess the innate intelligence to remember all things, but we can use a tool that is employed by many who practice the art of remembering things. The latter group informs us that the more absurd the association we make with the things we want to remember, the better our chances of remembering it.

In the case of the story I've mentioned, I have made the association of this story under the major heading of "Advice," but I've also embedded it in my mind by making the rather absurd association with Frank Lloyd Wright, the designer of the Tokyo Imperial Hotel, sitting in the lobby with water flowing through it. Now if I were asked to make comments before an architects' or builders' convention, or to make any reference concerning hotels, my mind would immediately recall for me the Frank Lloyd Wright story.

Let's take another example. Go to the section in the book under the major heading of "Agriculture & Gardening." The first story listed under this heading pertains to the Texas rancher who came to South Dakota to visit his farmer friend. In connection with my work I have spoken to many farm groups and organizations. This particular story when told is always well received by a rural audience. To be sure that I would always remember it, I have associated this particular story with a big Texan sitting at the wheel of a small dilapidated 1930 Model T Ford, and a rather smallish farmer sitting at his side. Having made this association, I have no difficulty in recalling the story for possible use whenever I address a group of agriculturalists, Texans, or even an automotive group.

The point to be made in the above two illustrations is that in order to remember things, unless you are especially gifted, you must make associations that enhance your recall abilities. The associations made under the major headings in this book or others that you might devise will be most helpful. Additionally, to imbed in your mind the things you really want to remember, make associations that are somewhat out of the ordinary — indeed absurd. If you do this you will soon surprise yourself with the great amount of material that you will readily recall which will be usable for you on many needed occasions.

ADVICE

Remember, when one points in accusation, three fingers point back at him.

****

Tell me your troubles
Your cares and your woes
And it won't cost you a dime
But when you're finished I will want to tell you mine.

****

A gardener weeding his plants on his knees was asked by a bystander if there was an easier way of doing it. "If there is," replied the gardener, "don't tell me. I like to suffer."

****

It sounds serious - take two aspirin and put your affairs in order.

****

Speak up. Make yourself vulnerable.

****

When you get too old to set a bad example you can always stick around and dish out good advice.

****

Mark Twain said, "Teach your son to cut his own wood, it will warm him twice."

****

Everyone should own a comfortable bed and comfortable pair of shoes because one spends most of his life in one or the other.

****

Before you decide to retire, stay home and watch some of the daytime TV programs.

****

The customer said "I'd like to get something for fleas." The clerk replied, "Go get a dog."

****

Strike the iron when it's hot, not when your head is hot.

****

Give not advice without being asked, and when desired do it briefly.

—George Washington

****

Frank Lloyd Wright, the famous architect, had designed a home for a client. Shortly after the home had been built, the client called Mr. Wright and said, "Mr. Wright, you know that home that you built for me? The roof is leaking and the basement is full of water. What shall I do?"

To which Mr. Wright replied, "Try to rise above it."

****

A lady had a problem with a skunk in her cellar. She called the local conservation officer. He said, "All you have to do is to spread a trail of bread crumbs from the basement on out and the skunk will follow it."

Two days later the lady called back and said, "I did what you told me, but now I have two skunks in my basement."

****

Make someone happy today—resign.

****

Lord, Lord, use me in Thy work—especially in an advisory capacity.

****

Wherever you go, there you are.

****

There's an old Chinese saying: "Give a man a fish and you feed him for a day. Teach him how to fish and you feed him for a lifetime."

****

AGRICULTURE & GARDENING

A Texas rancher, visiting a South Dakota farmer, asked him to show him his farm. After seeing the 1,000 acre spread, the Texan bragged that down home he could get into his car, drive all day, and by evening would not have gotten to the distant point of his ranch.

The South Dakotan simply replied, "You know, I had a car like that once."

****

Breathes there a gardener with a soul so dead
that to his neighbors have never said
"Here take a zucchini - they're great cooked or raw."
"What's that? You like them? Here, take ten more."
—Orben

****

What do you call a cow that has just had a calf? Decalfeinated.

3

****

A farmer was asked how he lost a couple of fingers on his hand. "Well," he said. "I put my hand into my horse's mouth to see how many teeth he had. He closed his mouth to see how many fingers I had."

****

A Pierre, South Dakota rancher sent his hired man to Texas to buy a special bull for his herd of Herefords. Having purchased the bull, the hired cowboy found he didn't have enough money to ship the bull back to South Dakota. So he went to the Western Union office to wire a message to his boss. The clerk informed the cowboy that his dollar and twenty-five cents would not be sufficient to send a message of more than three words, so the cowboy sent this message: "Com-fort-able."

****

Bumper sticker on a car in northwestern South Dakota: Eat lamb. One million coyotes can't be wrong.

****

The toughest speech I was ever called on to make was to a garden club the day after a heavy frost.

****

I bought a bag of fertilizer at the greenhouse and gave the clerk a check in payment. She rung it right up in her cash register. I said, "Aren't you going to check to see if it's okay?" "No," she said, "I know that crooks don't buy garden supplies."

****

Spring is here. The garage needs cleaning. Should we sweep it, clean it or plow it and plant it?

****

If Dolly Parton were a farmer she would be flat busted.

****

A farmer today is someone who makes his living from a second job.

****

A farmer went to see his veterinarian about his sick horse. The vet said, "Here, take these pills and give them to the horse." "How am I going to get the pills down the horse's throat," asked the farmer. He said, "You take this long tube, put the pills into it, put it into the horse's mouth and then blow." A couple days later the veterinarian saw his farmer friend and said, "How's the horse?" "Oh," he said, "the horse is doing okay, but I'm not doing so well." He said, "Well, what happened?" He said, "The horse blew first."

****

What do the Chinese call a calf? Yung cow.

****

Is the leather on this briefcase of good quality? "Yes," replied the clerk. "It held the cow together."

****

Farmers are
a hopeful set.
The more they farm
the less they net.

****

What did the cowboy say when he saw his horse come around a corner? Here comes my horse.

****

A farmer sent his water from his well to the State Laboratory to have it tested. Back came the report "Your horse has diabetes."

****

How bad was it during the 30's? My dad sold corn for three cents a bushel and oats for four cents less.

****

I lived on a farm where there were five boys and five girls, we milked thirty cows. We all pulled together.

****

If you want to teach your children frugality, become a plastic surgeon and cut their credit cards as they start out in life.

****

A rancher had trained his German Shepherd dog to be really ferocious and mean. Once going into a restaurant he was not allowed to take the dog inside, so he tied him up outside. While the rancher was eating, a person rushed in and asked who the owner of the big shepherd police dog was. The rancher promptly acknowledged that he was. The man then said "my Terrier just killed your dog." "Impossible." responded the rancher rather indignantly, "how could he kill my dog?" "Well, sir" he said, "my Terrier got in his throat."

****

A farmer is a man outstanding in his field.

****

My dad was no Burbank, but he was the first man to cross an Idaho potato with a sponge. It wasn't an especially good eating potato, but it sure held a lot of gravy.

****

The price of hogs had plummeted. Two farmers were discussing the situation. Said one, "if the price of hogs doesn't go up pretty soon, I'm going to have to rob a bank to make ends meet."

Whereupon his heavily mortgaged farmer friend replied, "I think I already have."

****

Pray for rain, but keep on hoeing.

****

The farmer is the first person to learn that there is no such thing as a free lunch.

****

Brigham Young said never steal a horse, for it costs more to hide it than it's worth.

****

A city man went out to visit his farmer friend. When he arrived at the farm, the farmer was hitching up his mule. The city man patted the mule on the back, and when he came to, the farmer said, "your intentions were good, but your approach was wrong."

****

A tourist traveling through South Dakota noticed the large number of cattle out in the pastures. He stopped and asked a native son, "How do you account for so many cattle in your state?"

"We prefer 'em," he replied.

****

A county agent is a person who knows enough to tell others how to farm, but is too smart to try it himself.

****

During the Depression, it was so dry that you were able to brand two calves at a time using carbon paper.

****

A rancher asked a veterinarian for some free advice. "I have a horse," he said, "that walks normally sometimes, and sometimes he limps. What shall I do?"

The veterinarian replied, "The next time he walks normally, sell him."

(—reprinted in *Readers Digest*)

****

There once was a red potato and a white potato. They got married and had a little sweet potato. When the little sweet potato grew up, she wanted to marry George Will, but her parents wouldn't allow it because Mr. Will was a common tater.

****

APPRECIATION

We make a living by what we get, but we make a life by what we give.

****

Wisdom is knowing what to do next.

****

The next time you think life is not worth living, stop and think of the alternative.

****

Men who do things that count never stop to count them.

****

Nothing becomes real until it becomes personal.

****

When I filled the gas tank in my old jalopy, it doubled in value.

****

Sign on a small foreign car: For sale or adoption.

****

Said the Reverend, "Detroit is not the only place where the maker can recall his product."

****

Do you want to make your house look bigger? Buy a small car and park out in front.

****

Yes, we do need safety belts for automobiles and an ejection seat for each backseat driver.

****

Having a four-wheel drive vehicle means that you can get stuck in more inaccessible places.

****

His car must have really been a gas guzzler. The filling station attendant asked him to shut it off for the reason that the car was getting ahead of him.

****

Said the mechanic to his customer "My advice to you is to keep the oil and change the car."

****

Good idea for a highway billboard "YOU ARE NOT WATCHING THE ROAD".

—Louie Warren

****

If you drive carelessly, your car will last you a lifetime.

****

"And how did you manage to run over that little sports car?"

"Well sir, I looked right and I looked left, but I plumb forgot to look down."

****

"Aren't you the fellow that sold me this car two weeks ago?"

"Yes, sir," said the salesman proudly.

"Well, then, tell me about it again. I get so discouraged."

****

The man who pokes fun at his wife for not being able to drive the car into the garage usually sobers up when he tries to thread a needle.

****

The other day I did what I've wanted to do ever since 1950—I bought myself a 1950 Cadillac!

****

My wife (husband) doesn't drive the car—she (he) aims it.

****

Our youngster parks cars by sound.

****

For that rundown feeling, try jaywalking.

****

Why in the world is it always the third car back that is the first to see the light turn green?

****

A motorist seeing a small sports car overturned on the side of the road brought his car to a screeching halt and then rushed over to ask the young man standing beside the overturned car, "Anybody hurt?"

The young man replied, "Heck, no. I'm just changing a tire."

****

"If you let me drive, I'll be an angel," she said. He did and she was.

****

AWARDS

My friend got the poultry award of the year for egg production by putting up a picture of Colonel Sanders in his chicken house.

****

BACHELOR

A bachelor farmer living with his mother had to make a trip to New York City. When he got there he called up his hired man to inquire as to how things were. "Well," replied the hired man, "I'm sorry to report that your cat, Tom, died." "Well, that disturbs me greatly" he told his hired man. "I wish you hadn't told me the bad news." "Well, what should I have done, boss?" the hired man inquired. "Well, you might have told me when I called in that Tom wasn't looking so good and the second time I called, you might have said that Tom was on the roof and so forth." "Okay Boss," replied the hired hand. "Incidentally," asked the bachelor, "How is mother?" "Well, she's on the roof."

—Ted Hustead of Wall Drug

****

There once was a cautious bachelor
who never romped nor played.
Who never smoked or drank
nor ever kissed a maid.
And when he up and passed away
his insurance was denied
for since he had never lived,
they claimed he never died.

****

A bachelor is a man with an un-alter-able view.

****

A bachelor is a man that comes to work from a different direction every morning.

****

A bachelor is a man who has not made the same mistake once.

****

A bachelor is a man who does not believe in feathering his own nest.

****

BALDNESS AND BARBERS

In one of his sermons our pastor stated that God knows everyone by name, the day you were born, the day you were baptized into the kingdom, the number of hairs on your head, etc. When I came home, I looked at myself in the mirror—at my thinning hair and concluded that the Lord's responsibility over me was greatly diminished.

****

I have a joke that will knock the hair right off of your head. Oh, wait, I see that you've already heard it.

****

One thing you can say for baldness is that it is neat.

****

Some have to come out on top to set shining examples.

****

Old barbers never die, they just can't cut it like they used to.

****

If you're losing a little on the top, cheer up. You're probably gaining it back in the middle.

****

Just because there is no snow on the roof does not mean that there is no fire in the furnace.

****

Research shows that baldness at the back of the head indicates a thinker; baldness at the front of the head a lover; and a man who is bald all over just thinks he's a lover.

****

Looking at my bald head makes me think of heaven—there is no parting there.

****

When the Lord makes something good, He doesn't cover it up.

****

A sign of wealth is when a bald man gets a haircut.

****

BANKING

Way down South
in the Land of Cotton
Overdrafts are soon forgotten.
          —Burt Lance, Jimmy Carter's Administration

****

Robbers held up a country bank and scooped up every coin in sight. Just as they were getting ready to leave, the teller called back to one of the bandits and said "Do me a favor. Take the books too, I'm about $500 short."

****

Ozzie went down to see our banker and told him that he had good and bad news. The banker inquired, "What's the bad news?" Ozzie replied, "We won't be able to pay interest on our loan this year, nor the principal." The banker then asked, "Well, what's the good news?" Ozzie stated, "Al and I have decided to stick with you one more year."

****

He is not a bigot. He hates everyone.

****

A man went to the hospital to have his leg amputated. When he came out of surgery he asked the surgeon "How did it go?" The surgeon replied, "I have both good news and bad news." "Well," he said, "give me the bad news first." "We made a mistake and cut off your good leg." "Now give me the good news," replied the patient. "Your bad leg is getting better."

****

A friend said to his buddy that he got married a year ago. "Well," said his friend "that was good." "No," said he, "she was a crabby old woman." "Well," he said "that was bad." "No," he said, "that was good, she had a lot of money." "Well, that was good" said his friend. "No," he said "that was bad, she wouldn't let me spend it. But she had a nice house." "Well, that was good, wasn't it." "No, that was bad, it burned down." "Well, that was certainly too bad." "No that was good, she was in it."

****

A born loser as reported by Paul Harvey - "A man in New York took the cover off a manhole to crash a window at a jewelry store and then he stepped back to admire his success and dropped into the manhole."

****

The business man who starts a hog farm in Israel.

****

The person who absent-mindedly raises the thermostat in his own wax museum.

****

The hitchhiker who was sucking his thumb when a car went by.

****

The window washer who steps back to admire his own work.

****

BOSS

A man was astounded one morning to read an announcement of his death in the newspaper. He rushed to his phone and called up his boss and said "Hello, did you see the announcement of my death in the newspaper?" "Yes," the boss replied "Where are you calling from?"

****

The reason the boss had an open door policy was because he couldn't afford a lock.

****

In my house I am the boss, I wear the pants. Of course they are protected with an apron.

****

I'm just like the rest of you around here—just a number. The only difference is that I'm number one.

****

A good boss is a person who takes a little more than his share of the blame and a little less than his share of the credit.

****

16

A boss who gets to work at 8 a.m. and opens all his own mail must have something to conceal.

****

Boss: "I have good news for all of the employees today. We have complied with all federal, state and local regulations. All forms have been completed and sent in. I also have some bad news — the company is filing for bankruptcy."

****

BUSINESS

With skirts getting shorter, the end of the recession is finally in sight.

****

Truth in Advertising
I saw a beggar with a sign, "I could be blind".

****

The sure formula for failure is to start a tall man's shop in Tokyo.

****

The Romans had a hard time making money. The lions ate all of their prophets.

****

The rules of employment at this particular firm were so tough that they only allowed one day to attend a funeral and that was your own.

****

Success comes by doing successfully one thing at a time.

****

Economists have forecast twelve of the last four recessions.

****

The judge presiding over a bankruptcy hearing opened the meeting by reading from the book of Revelation, chapter 11.

****

It's important for man to have a wife because when things go wrong he can't blame everything on the federal government.

****

Seven-elevens in the Bahamas are called nine and tens. That is because they may open at nine or they may open at ten.

****

Do you want a box for your groceries? The customer said, "I'd rather not."

****

"Dear, you look awfully tired today. Is there something the matter?" "Yes," replied the husband, "today I took an aptitude test and believe me, it's a good thing that I run the company."

****

The sign in a Volkswagen salesroom said, "Think big and you're fired."

****

The balance sheet as shown on a company's annual report was padded with enough good will to ensure permanent world peace.

****

If we learn from our mistakes and failures, you and I, Ozzie, should have a bright future.

****

One wonders if the man who invented lifesavers really made a mint.

****

A Census Bureau questionnaire, "Give us a list of your employees broken down by sex." Businessman, "I don't know."

****

FINAL CUT

The most discouraging of business news,
It should hardly be surprising,
Is having a one man consulting firm,
And finding that it needs downsizing.
—Edward F. Dempsey

****

He was very entrepreneurial — sounds like a disease doesn't it?

****

Would it make for a bad image if the Otis Elevator Company had its main office on the first floor?

****

Every business has its problems, but there is no problem like no business.

****

A customer came into the supermarket near closing. She asked the butcher for a nice chicken. He brought one out, put it on the scale and said it weighed three and a half pounds. She wanted a larger one. He stepped back into the cooler and discovered that there were no more. So he brought the original chicken back out and said, "Ma'am, I've got one here that's almost four pounds."

"That will do," she said. "I'll take them both."

****

A recession is a period when you tighten your belt. A depression is a time when you have no belt to tighten. When you have no trousers to hold up, man, that's a panic.

****

The counselor asked the employee how long he had been working at the company. He said, "Ever since they tried to fire me."

****

How to succeed in business without really trying? Embezzle company funds.

****

A merchant was having his sales clerk stock some shelves. The clerk noticed that the invoice cost was $1 per unit and he was asked to put a sales price of $4 on each item. "Boss," he said, "isn't that taking too much of a markup?" "What's wrong with three percent?" fired back his employer.

****

The young executive came home and told his wife that he had just been made vice president at the bank. She said, "Oh, that's nothing. They have so many vice presidents now that down at the grocery store where I shop, they even have a vice president in charge of the prune department." He didn't believe her, so she said, "Why don't you call the grocery store?" He called and asked the person who answered, "Will you please give me the vice president of the prune department?"

Back came the response, "Bulk or packaged?"

****

The reverend was admonishing his parishioners on the evils of sin.

"Remember, my friends," he said, "there will be no buying or selling in heaven." A disgruntled old gent in the back row shouted back, "That's not where business is going, anyway."

****

An executive is that type of person who solves more problems than he creates.

****

Our government states that it is a 50-50 partner with business. Sometimes I wish it would choose another partner.

****

We are expecting another baby—business is expanding on all fronts.

****

There's a lot of free cheese in mousetraps, but you don't find any happy mice there.

****

To err is human, to forgive is against company policy.

****

Who's afraid of recessions? I've failed during boom times.

****

A desk is a wastebasket with drawers.

****

CAPITAL PUNISHMENT

Anyone who believes in capital punishment ought to be hanged.

****

The man condemned to die in the electric chair asked his minister if he had any parting words of wisdom for him. Whereupon the reverend replied, "Yes, don't sit down."

****

As the minister was leaving the execution chamber, the condemned man implored him to please hold his hand.

****

The cure for crime is not the electric chair, but the high chair.

****

CHARISMA

Nonchalance:
The ability to look like an owl when you've behaved like an ass.

****

He has so much charm that when he tells you to go to Hell you can't wait to get started.

****

Charm is something people have until they begin to rely upon it.

****

Charm and wit and levity
May help one at the start,
But in the end it's brevity
That wins the public's heart.

—Anonymous

****

CHILDREN AND GRANDCHILDREN STORIES

I resemble that remark.

—Garfield

****

A boy was fishing on the dock through a small hole. "You must be a dumb nut," said his older friend. "You can't bring a big fish in through that hole." "No, you're dumb." "The big fish I intend to catch can't pull me through."

****

What did one slice of bread say to the other slice?
You're pretty crumby.

****

A lady asked a young boy, "If you had five pieces of candy and I asked for two of them, how many would you have left?" Answered the young boy, "five".

****

Our children have all the faults that we have outgrown.

****

"Dear, would you take Junior to the zoo?" " No, dear, if they want him, they can come and get him."

****

Twerpies is a canarial disease of canaries that can't tweep.

****

He who is without sin shall cast out the first stoned.

****

We have five children - all white. That's remarkable considering that three out of every five babies born in the world today are Asian.

****

"Grandpa," asked the granddaughter, "make a sound like a frog." Her grandpa said, "I can't, but I can make a sound like a cow." "Why not like a frog?" inquired the granddaughter. "Why do you want me to make a sound like a frog?" asked grandpa. "Because grandma says that as soon as you croak we can go to Hawaii."

****

To clean up after children
while they are growing
is like shoveling the sidewalk
while it is still snowing.

****

"There's a fork in the road," said Lauren to her grandpa. "Let's eat."

****

A doctor cautioned the old man that he should no longer shovel sidewalks. Along came a heavy snowfall and the father asked his son to shovel the sidewalk. The son replied, "Sure, Dad." Then the Dad fell over from a heart attack.

****

The teacher said to the pupils, "If you have to go to the bathroom, just hold up your hand." Replied one of the pupils, "How is that going to help, teacher?"

****

There once was a lady named Har
Who kept her two sons in a jar
She said she wasn't mean
but it kept her house clean
As long as they stayed where they are.

****

He was as confused as a little boy who lost his chewing gum in the chicken coop.

****

I slept like a baby last night. I woke up every two hours.

****

A mother kept reminding her young son to wash his hands because of germs. One day he was overheard mumbling, "All I ever hear about is germs and Jesus and I've not seen either."

****

Should kids wearing baggy pants to school be suspendered?

****

Why aren't elephants permitted on the beach? It's because they won't keep their trunks up.

****

An irritated elderly lady asked a sniffling boy seated next to her on the bus, "Young man, don't you have a handkerchief?" "Yes," he said, "but I don't lend it to strangers."

****

Have I told you about my grandchildren? No, and I appreciate it, too.

****

"I never censor or berate my children.
When they've incensed me
I'm fearful, lest they'll
Demonstrate against me."

****

If the kids become suddenly all quiet in the house, the parents should begin to worry.

****

A young man inquired of his father when he saw a wanted poster in the post office. "Why didn't they nab him when they took his picture."

****

A newspaper boy sent a Christmas card to one of his customers. Two weeks later came another Christmas card and scribbled on it was "Second Notice".

****

A lion ambling through the jungle came upon a fox and inquired, "Who is King of the Jungle?" The fox replied, "You are". Then the lion ran into a monkey and again inquired, "Who is King of the Jungle?" The monkey quickly replied, "You are, Mr. Lion." The he came upon a huge elephant and again inquired, "Who is King of the Jungle?" Where upon the elephant took his trunk and slung him up a tree. As the lion slithered down, he said to the elephant, "You don't have to be so darned mad just because you didn't know the right answer."

****

A grandfather told his grandson that at his age he thought nothing of getting up at five o'clock in the morning. The grandson replied to the grandfather "Yes, and I don't think much of it either."

****

We just can't give into terrorists. Anyone who has had children knows that.

****

His parents didn't have any money so he was born at home. When his mother saw him she had to be taken to the hospital.

****

The young son was standing on his head and his father inquired, "Andrew, why are you standing on your head?" "Oh," replied Andrew, "I'm just turning things over in my mind."

****

The father said to his son, "I taught you everything I know and you're still ignorant."

****

Grandson to Grandma, "Your stockings are wrinkled, Grandma." "I'm not wearing stockings," replied Grandma.

****

My grandson, Kyle, asked me, "What did one kangaroo say to the other kangaroo?" "Beats me," I said. Then he replied, "I'm so hoppy to see you."

****

Teacher: Spell straight.
Pupil: Straight.
Teacher: That's correct, what does it mean?
Pupil: Without water.

****

When you are a young parent you check out the movies that you want your kids to see, and when you get older the kids check out the movies you should see.

****

A night is something to get the children through.

****

The Boy Scout came to his troop meeting with a black eye. When asked what had happened, he said that he had tried to help an elderly lady across the street. "How in the world," asked the Scoutleader, "did you get a black eye doing that?" "Well," the young Scout replied, "she didn't want to go."

****

The Sunday School teacher told her class, "Now children, I want you to be so quiet that you can hear a pin drop."

After a few seconds of total quiet, a little boy yelled, "Okay, teacher, let her drop."

****

Spank your children every day. If you don't know what for, they will.

****

If your children don't consider you an embarrassment at an early age, they don't have proper parents. (from M.S. Forbes)

****

I told my young boy to go to the end of the line, but he came back and said, "Dad, there's someone already there."

****

Little children, little trouble; big children, big trouble.

****

Kids don't go to camp, they are sent there.

****

The easiest children to bring up are calm, thoughtful, and somebody else's.

****

The number of perfect children in the world is directly proportional to the number of average parents.

****

CIVIL RIGHTS

"What do you think of the Civil Rights Bill?" asked the constituent of his congressman. He replied, "If we owe it, I think we ought to pay it."

****

COMMITTEES AND CONVENTIONS

She sent me to the convention with my conscience while she stayed home flirting with her imagination.

****

There was a fellow who said he left his wife at home because it cost him half as much and he had twice as much fun.

****

If you're a delegate-at-large to a convention that means that your spouse did not accompany you.

****

Committees are good weapons for killing time.

****

A government study ended by stating, "the overwhelming conclusion is that no conclusion could be drawn."

****

The unable appointed by the unwilling to do the unnecessary.

****

The camel is a horse that was put together by a committee.

****

God so loved the world that he did not leave it in the hands of a committee.

****

COMMUNICATION

"Why," inquired the newcomer to the city, "are there so many people named Smith in the telephone book?" Replied the local resident, "Could it be that they all have telephones?"

****

A lady asked an artist whether he would paint her in the nude. He said, "Yes," provided he could keep his socks on.

****

Why are there so few telephones in China? It's because there are too many people with surnames with Wing and Wong and so people are always afraid of winging the wong number.

****

A gentleman desirous of obtaining a parrot that could speak two languages kept searching for several months. One day the operator of the local pet shop called him and said that he had just such a parrot. On arriving at the pet shop, the operator informed the prospective customer that the parrot spoke not two languages, but five. He was delighted. So he said, "Just send the cage and the parrot to my home. My wife will be there to receive it."

When the purchaser arrived at home at six o'clock that evening, he asked his wife, "What is for dinner?"

"You should ask," she replied. "you sent it home this afternoon."

"Do you mean to tell me, dear, that you cooked the parrot that I sent home? The one I've been searching for for such a long time? And did you know that the parrot could speak not only two languages, but five?"

"Why, then," asked the wife, "didn't he speak up?"

****

Advertising pays, but there is no sense in advertising our troubles. There is no market for them.

****

On the big island of Hawaii, game officials discovered that the mongoose was a predator of the rat. An official on a neighboring island, having a rat problem, felt that he should like to import a pair of mongooses. So he wrote a letter to the game official on the big island. He started out by stating, "Dear Sir, will you please send me two mongeese."

Thinking that his English was not correct, he tore it up and gave it a second try. This time he wrote, "Dear Sir, will you please send me two mongeeses?" This still didn't sound quite right, so he tore it up once more and gave it a third try. This time he wrote, "Dear Sir, will you please send me one mongoose. Thank you very much. Sincerely."

Then he signed it, adding this P.S.: "Aw, shucks, inasmuch as you're sending me one, why don't you throw another one in the box?"

****

COMMUNISM

There is a new organization in Russia called the UFFR.
—The Union of Fewer and Fewer Republics. - 1991.

****

Mohammed Ali returned from Russia during the peak of the Communistic rule. He stated he found no prostitutes, no guns, no crimes, and no gays. In response, Al Ableson wrote: "How could anyone be gay in so dreary a place."

****

A man with a terminal illness joined the Communistic party. When asked why, he said it was better that one of them should go.

****

When I was in East Berlin in 1959, they had a huge statue of Stalin in Lenin Square. I heard someone remark "It was so huge that it provided shade in the summer, protection from the winds and elements in the winter and gave birds and opportunity to speak for everyone."

****

COMPLIMENTS

Smiley Burnett quotes:
1. "It's nice to be important, but it's more important to be nice."
2. "The smaller the depot, the bigger the agent."
3. "There are three types of people that live in the city, (a.) those that live in the town, (b.) those that live off the town and (c.) those that live for the town."

4."Money won't make you happy, it will just keep you comfortable while you're unhappy."

****

Though the distance between the two is only 11 inches, the results received from a pat on the back or a kick in the pants are vastly different.

****

You get most credit by giving credit to those whom credit is due.

****

Flattery will not hurt you so long as you don't inhale it.

****

DAIRY

Ad: "Wanted: dairy employee with no bad habits such as drinking, smoking or eating margarine."

****

If you want to cry over spilled milk, condense it.

****

For two decades there has been considerable talk about the high cholesterol content of foods. In the mid-50's, Dr. Ancel Keyes was a great proponent of low cholesterol diets and implicated dairy products as being high in cholesterol content. Following is one dairyman's reply:
"We all have to go, Dr. Keyes,
But the guy with the heart goes with ease,
So why give up butter and cheese
And wait for some ghastly disease?"

****

Milk is the only liquid that has enough sense to sour naturally.

****

Why is it that Swiss cheese has all the holes when it's limburger that needs the ventilation?

****

Two cows in a pasture near a highway saw a tank truck pass by with a sign on the side reading, "Pasteurized, homogenized, standardized, and vitamin D added."

One turned to the other and remarked, "Makes you feel sort of inadequate, doesn't it?"

****

"How do you put those holes into Swiss cheese?"
"It's easy, we just use whole milk."

****

That's udderly ridiculous.

****

I should like to hear the udder side.

****

Smile when you say "cheese."

****

Milk: The udder cola.

****

You can make cheese at home, for where there's a will there's a whey.

****

A Quaker was milking his cow when she switched her tail, hitting him in the eye and causing a severe burning sensation. The cow had done this several times. He could stand it no longer so he set down his bucket, went around the stanchion and stood directly in front of the cow and said, "Thou knowest that I canst smite thee. But what thou does not know is that I can sell thee to my Lutheran friend, and he can beat the holy h— out of you."

****

DECISIONS

I don't hate anyone. I do have a few on my list just in case I change my mind.

****

Many of the toughest decisions of life are made in the bathroom - when to discard a toothpaste tube that's nearly empty, a worn-out toothbrush or razor blade or a sliver of soap.

****

Indecision is a form of hell on earth.

****

Learn to make decisions quickly but be careful in giving your reasons. Your decisions are often right, but your reasons are wrong.

****

Decide and be done with it.

****

Decide—make yourself vulnerable.

****

Washington had a wooden tooth. He brushed his teeth once a day and saw his carpenter twice a year.

****

The dentist's bill for pulling a tooth was fifty bucks. The patient asked if that wasn't a high hourly rate for such a short period of time. "Well, maybe, yes," said the dentist. "I could have pulled it more slowly."

****

Dear Ann Landers, I'm a red head and I'm about to be married. One thing bothers me. I have a set of false teeth. Should I tell him? Sincerely yours, Frannie.

Dear Frannie, Marry him and keep your mouth shut.

****

If you want to save your teeth, mind your own business.

****

Do you promise to pull the tooth, the whole tooth, and nothing but the tooth?

****

Teeth are very nice to have,
They fill you with content;
If you do not know it now,
You will when they have went!

****

"Mom, I can't brush my teeth. The battery is dead."

****

The reason Mahatma Gahndi was so thin
Was that Weight Watchers simply forgot to say when.

****

We brew our coffee the old-fashioned way. We urn it.

****

This food is so bad I'm thinking about a cookout - going into the kitchen and telling the cook "out."

****

At Thanksgiving time, the young child told her mother, "I don't like the stuffing in this turkey. I wonder why the turkey ate it."

****

I'm on a seafood diet - Whenever I see food, I eat it.

****

The coffee was so weak that I had to help it out of the spout.

****

How do you like that for a diet? Well, it's not half bad. It's all bad.

****

H_1O is fat-free water.

****

Mahatma Gandhi was the only man that got out of bed in the morning and took a sheet with him.

****

His wife was so bad that her cooking set off the fire alarm.

****

A customer ordered lamb chops and when they came he told the waitress, "Gee these are small." Later when the waitress came back he said to her, "They didn't taste too good either." Then the waitress said, "Now aren't you thankful that they were small?"

****

I read where carrot juice is good for one's eyes, so I drank a lot of it. The only problem was that I was ultimately able to see through my eyelids and lost a lot of sleep.

****

"Breakfast is a lovely meal,
Which for me has great appeal.
I like the smell of coffee most,
But oh the sight of golden toast,
With two fresh eggs superbly fried,
and crispy bacon at their side.
And fruit according to the season,
Almost makes me lose my reason.
Breakfast, breakfast you can't beat it,
Someday I hope you'll have time to eat it."

—Author Unknown

****

Then there was a fast food place that ran into financial trouble because too many of its customers were slow eaters.

****

There is a new diet that is very effective. You only eat when there's good news.

****

There's a new Chinese diet out: Eat all you want, but you're allowed only one chopstick.

****

I got on the scale and it said, "Come back when you're alone."

****

The best way to diet is to keep your mouth shut and your refrigerator closed.

****

My wife is on a diet where she's losing five pounds per week. I've calculated in 30 weeks I'll be completely rid of her.

****

There's a new diet called the sample diet—you can taste all the food you want to, but if it tastes good, you have to spit it out.

****

My wife is on a diet where she eats all she wants to one day and then she fasts for two days. It's called the rhythm method of girth control.

****

My doctor has just put me on a new diet. He told me that I could eat anything that I liked, and then he gave me a list of the foods that I like.

****

The dieter asked the waiter, "Is this plate damp?"
"No," was the reply, "that's your soup."

****

"How did you find your steak?"
"It was easy. I moved the potato over, and there it was."

****

A diet is for people who are thick and tired of it.

****

The hardest part of a diet is not watching what you eat— it's watching what others eat.

****

I'm in good shape for the shape that I'm in.

DRINKING

A slightly intoxicated customer buying additional liquor at a liquor store and intending to pay with a credit card was asked to identify himself. He stepped in the front of the mirror and then told the clerk, "Yup, that's me".

****

"Do you drink to excess," inquired the officer. "No sir" replied the slightly intoxicated man. "I'll drink to anything."

****

Sometimes too much drink is not enough.

****

If two old maids sat on the bleachers with a fifth of scotch, what inning would it be? The end of the fifth with the bags loaded.

****

The lady was shocked to find two empty liquor bottles in her garbage. Afraid the garbage man might think she was drinking, she took the two empty bottles and put them into the minister's garbage next door. She rationalized that everyone knew that the minister didn't drink.

****

A driver who has one for the road in all possibility will have a patrolman as a chaser.

****

"I can't find the reason for your illness," said the Doctor to the patient, "however it may be due to drinking." Replied the patient, "OK Doc, I'll come back when you are sober."

****

"If I were as drunk and in your condition," said the lady to the highly intoxicated fellow, "I'd shoot myself." Came back the reply, "If you were in my condition, lady, you'd miss."

****

A horse went into a bar, sat on the stool and ordered a drink.

A very drunk fellow on the next stool turned and asked of the horse, "Why do you have such a long face?"

****

There was a bar that was so cheap, they had a Happy Minute.

****

Do you have any Christmas cheer in this house? Well, let me look into my liquor cabinet.

****

Did you hear about the fella that killed a fifth of scotch at five a.m. and then attended Mass. What's so great about that? Well, the fellow was Jewish.

****

A husband had a real drinking problem and frequently came home drunk. One night his wife decided to meet him at the door when he arrived home. Just as the husband reached for the door knob she pulled it open and the husband fell flat on his face. "What do you have to say for yourself?" she asked. He looked up at her and said, "I don't come with a prepared statement but I'll take questions from the floor."

****

The judge asked the defendant why he would drive a car when he was in such an intoxicated condition. "Well sir," replied the defendant, "I was just too drunk to walk."

****

Did you hear about the government program called Bourbon Renewal: you take one drink and the whole town looks better.

****

In one western city when one gets four DWIs, he can turn them in for a bicycle.

****

He no longer attends Alcoholics Anonymous. He just sends them the empties.

****

The airline stewardess asked the Reverend passenger if he'd like a drink. "No," he replied. "I'm too close to the main office."

****

Life's been sweet to me
I've had fun galore
I'd rather have the morning after
Than to have missed the night before.

****

A police officer using a breathalizer on a drunk driver said, "This is a machine that tells how much alcohol is in your blood." Replied the drunk driver, "You didn't have to buy one, I married one."

****

At a cocktail party the husband said to his wife, "Don't take another drink, honey, your face is getting blurred."

****

"Were you in the Air Force?"
"No I was just a test pilot for Seagrams."

****

The bus driver asked one of his regular passengers, "Did you get home okay last night?"
"Yeah, why?"
"You got up to give a lady your seat and you were the only one on the bus."

****

He said to his brother, "I hear that you may be drinking too much." "Oh no," he said, "not to worry, in my home-town there are a lot of people who are a lot worse off than I am and none of them drink."

****

Then there was the fellow who went on a drinking man's diet, he didn't lose any weight just his driver's license.

****

Then did you hear the one about the (your nationality) that climbed up on the roof because he heard that the drinks were on the house.

****

A man was flagged down for speeding, but he argued with the patrol officer, "I know that I've not been speeding." The argument with the officer went on for a few minutes then his wife leaned forward and said, "Officer, it's no use to argue with my husband when he's been drinking."

****

Two buddies were drinking heavily. "I'm hungry" said the one and reached to get an olive out of the other's martinis. Then he said "This calls for an after-dinner drink."

****

"The way to become an alcoholic," said the confirmed drunkard, "is to take a drink and then you feel like a new man, and then he needs a drink."

****

The professor was demonstrating before his class the ill effects of alcohol. He took a worm and dropped it into a beaker of water. The worm just continued to wiggle about. Then he dropped the worm into a beaker of alcohol and immediately the worm died. Then he asked the class what that proved. A young man replied, "Professor, that just proves that people that drink don't have worms."

****

A drunk got lost in a cemetery on his way home. When he woke up he asked himself, "If I'm alive, why am I lying here among the tombstones? If I'm dead, why do I have to go to the bathroom?"

****

An announcement from the emcee: "Sir, I've just been informed that your coat in the lobby is leaking."

****

In our mountain country in Kentucky it is hard to eke out the bare necessities, and often they're not even fit to drink.

****

A drunk was walking with one foot in the gutter and one on the sidewalk. "My," said a passerby, "you must be drunk."

"Thank God," said the drunk, "I thought I was a cripple."

****

The liquor truck ran over my Scotchman friend. It was the first time that the drinks were on him.

****

A universal joint is a tavern in outer space.

****

It's okay to drink like a fish if you drink what the fish drinks.

****

Small fry to father: "How come soda pop will spoil my dinner and martinis give you an appetite?"

****

I was insulted when my friend offered me a drink so I drank his insult.

****

EDUCATION

Lincoln came from abject poverty. He walked nine miles to get books from the library. Now we close the libraries on his birthday.

****

A teacher said to her pupils, "If I lay four eggs here and three there, how many will I have?"

One of her students replied, "Teacher, I don't think you can do it."

****

Teacher: "If you had nine dollars in one pocket in your pants and ten dollars in the other pocket, how much money would you have?"

Student: "None."

Teacher: "Why?"

Student: "Well, they wouldn't be my pants."

****

The mother said to her son, "Get up, it's time for school." Yelled back her son, "Give me three good reasons why I should get up and go to school."

"First," she said, "You are fifty years old. Secondly, education is important to the nation and thirdly, you are the principal."

****

He had so many degrees that his middle name was called "Fahrenheit".

****

The teacher asked one of her students, "Which is farthest — the moon or the English Channel?" "Teacher," responded the pupil, "it must be the moon because we cannot get the English Channel on our TV set."

****

Teacher: "Do you know Lincoln's Gettysburg Address?"

Student: "No, did he move?"

****

You must be an old timer when you can remember that sex education was available only behind the schoolhouse and not in it.

****

Fourth grade student to his teacher, "My dad said that if my grades don't get any better someone's going to get a whipping."

****

A doctor can bury his mistakes; an architect can cover them up; a farmer can plow them under, but a teacher's mistakes may grow up and become members of school boards.

****

A biology teacher asked his class how do lions make love. Replied a young lad in the rear of the room, "I don't know, my dad is a Rotarian."

****

There are doctors of philosophy, doctors of science, doctors of theology, doctors of this and that. The prefix "doctor" has about as much meaning as the curl in a pig's tail. It doesn't add anything to the value of the hog, but it sure tickles the ham.

****

I once had two teachers—one had no principle, and the other had no class.

****

Life is a risk,
Nothing is sure,
Except for the professor
Who's got his tenure.

****

"Education is a good thing, and blessed is the person who has it."

—Brigham Young

****

EGOTISM

Humility is not one of my faults; but if I had one, that would be it.

****

I'm not egotistical-but what a blessing it was that I was born.

****

I seldom ever make a mistake. I thought I made one once, but I was wrong.

****

Please don't sit too close to me. People have been scorched by my talent.

****

Our speaker this evening is a legend in his own mind.

****

I asked a Texan one time where Lubbock County was and he said, "In the northwest corner of my ranch."

****

Egotists are self-made men. They worship their creator.

****

Egotists
When two egotists get together,
This you cannot deny,
It's not a tooth for a tooth,
But an I for an I.

****

He was so conceited that when he calls Dial-A-Prayer he asks for messages.

****

I used to be the most egotistical man in my home town. Then I went to see a psychiatrist and now I'm just the nicest guy in town.

****

ELECTRICIANS

Old electricians never die—they just get defused.

****

Two repairmen were working on the power lines in front of the widow's home. The repair work required some soldering using hot metal. Inadvertently, the man at the top of the pole spilled some hot solder and it hit his buddy on the back of the neck, slid down his back, and out the bottom of his pants leg. There was a profuse and immediate outburst of profanity directed by the victim against his buddy doing the repair work. The widow was shocked by it all and called the power company officials to complain about the abusive language that had been used.

The two workmen were called in to explain exactly what happened. The man doing the soldering said, "I accidentally dropped some of the hot metal. Unfortunately, it hit Jim who was standing at the bottom of the pole."

"What," asked the manager, "did you do, Jim?"

"Well," he said, "I just looked up at Bob and I said, 'Bob, you must never allow that to happen again'."

****

EMCEEING

This is going to be a very brief introduction because there are not too many good things to say about our speaker.

****

A man was being introduced as a very successful businessman. The introducer pointed out that the guest speaker had made a million dollars in Texas oil. When he got up to speak, he thanked the introducer for the introduction, but said, "I have to set the facts straight concerning the million dollars the introducer referred to. It wasn't oil," he stated, "it was coal, and it wasn't in Texas it was in Oklahoma and it wasn't a million dollars it was just a $100,000 and it wasn't me but it was my brother and he didn't make it, he lost it."

****

Should we allow the audience to enjoy themselves a little longer, or should I introduce you now?

****

Some bring happiness wherever they go, others whenever they go.

****

If you have been looking for someone lousy—I'm it.

****

I'm a self-made man. That relieves the Lord of all responsibility.

****

The introduction was better than I expected, but worse than I deserved.

****

Laugh a little faster. Time is short.

****

Careful research has shown that it takes an emcee 10 minutes to introduce a man that needs no introduction.

****

You may now raise your eyes and look upon me.

****

Responding to the introducer: "May the Lord forgive you for the perjury you have just committed. But on the other hand, I hope that all the rest of you will accept it as Holy Writ."

****

I have a photographic mind. I've just never had it developed.

****

Always be sincere even if you don't mean it.

****

It's nice to be among friends, even if you are not mind.

****

I feel like a fugitive from the law of averages.

****

Women need no introduction. They can speak for themselves.

****

I would like to say that this is the brightest audience that I have ever appeared before—but I can't.

****

This is certainly a dense—I mean large crowd.

****

After the audience applauds, you might say, "I wish I had your confidence."

****

You're my kind of audience — trapped!

****

Talk is cheap. The supply is larger than the demand.

****

I asked the speaker whether he was married. His reply, "Guilty."

****

ENVIRONMENT AND ECOLOGY

I think I shall never see
A billboard lovely as a tree
Perhaps if the billboards do not fall
I'll never see a tree at all.

—Ogden Nash

****

Two young biologists were sent to Alaska by the Bureau of Sports & Fisheries to study terns, a native bird of Alaska. The two men had been in Alaska about a month and still had not caught a tern so they could research its habits. So they decided to place out a saucer with vodka for the birds to drink. Sure enough the experiment worked. The terns showed up, drank some of the alcohol and became intoxicated. Thus it became possible for the biologist to capture the terns they needed for their studies. When they sent their final report into Washington D. C. the last sentence in the report said, "we left no tern unstoned."

****

A congressman's speech on the environment sure muddied up the water.

****

Unless you're the lead dog on a dog sled team, the scenery never changes.

****

I dropped my watch into some flea powder, it killed all the ticks.

****

The smog in (__city__) is so bad that a friend of mine shot an arrow into the air and it stuck right there.

****

That stream is so turbid that there are fish in it that are three years old and still don't know how to swim.

****

Here's my report card, Dad, and it's bad again. What do you suppose is the matter with me anyway, heredity or environment?

****

All those in favor of saving gas, raise your right foot.

****

The most common insect found around these parts is the litterbug.

****

EPITAPHS

An inscription of the tombstone read, "I always told them I wasn't feeling well."

****

A sailor placing some flowers on a grave in a cemetery noticed an old Chinaman placing a bowl of rice on a nearby grave and asked, "What time do you expect your friend to come up and eat the rice?" The Chinaman replied, "The same time your friend comes up to smell the flowers."

****

Epithet on a tombstone in the cemetery, "Excuse me for not rising."

****

The atheist says, "While you live,
live in clover,
because when you are dead
you're dead all over."

****

It isn't the cough
That sends you off.
It's the coffin
They send you off-in.

****

Long after I have disappeared
In time's eternal mists
I know my name will still remain
On all the sucker lists.

—Jane Saunders

****

ETHNIC STORIES

Note to the Reader: In some of the following ethnic stories we have left blanks so that if you wish to use this type of story you can fill in the name of the nationality most prevalent in your area.

Ole and Lena farmed Southwest of Minneapolis. They hadn't visited the city in years. Said Ole to Lena one morning, "Let's go to Minneapolis tomorrow and watch that Lions International Parade." So off they went. Upon arriving in Minneapolis, Ole promptly got a ticket for driving the wrong direction in a one-way street. Then he got a second ticket for parking in a place reserved for the handicapped. This was followed with a third ticket for going thirty-five miles an hour in a twenty-five mile an hour speed zone. "Lena," said Ole, "I don't think these Minneapolis people like us. Let's go home."

"Okay with me," said Lena. Heading out of the city there was a huge billboard with the lettering KOA. Then said Lena to Ole, "And they can kiss ours, too."

****

Ole worked on the Alaskan Highway and had not seen Lena for months. One day he asked his boss if he could go

56

home to Minneapolis to visit Lena. His request was granted, so Ole skied all the way back to Minneapolis. Folks in Minneapolis were so impressed that they sent a reporter to interview Ole. "What's the first thing you did when you got home?" inquired the reporter.

"I made love to Lena," replied Ole.

"Well, we can't print that," replied the reporter. "What's the second thing you did?"

"Well, I made love to Lena."

"No, no Ole, I don't think you understand." "Tell me, what is the third thing you did?"

"Well, sir, I took off my skis."

****

What do you get when you cross a Norwegian with a German? A fisherman who wants to rule the roost.

****

There is a continuing argument whether it was the Scandinavians or Columbus who first discovered America. Maybe this will shed some light on it. When Columbus left to return to Spain, one of the natives said, "When you get home, greet the Ericksons for us."

****

There are basically two types of people in this world - Scandinavians and those who would like to be.

****

The Norwegian said to his Swedish friend, "You Swedes have many things to brag about including the fact that you have better neighbors."

****

Rueben Goertz, a noted historian of Mennonite people stated that Highway 81, which passes through several states including South Dakota and North Dakota is called a Mennonite Holy Highway.

****

The Mennonites have had a reputation of being very frugal. One day a shop keeper had a Mennonite for a customer. The Mennonite had a ten dollar bill in one hand and the Ten Commandments in the other and vowed not to break either.

****

Did you hear about (ethnic nationality) that loved his wife so much, he almost told her once.

****

If you see three Santas on the roof, how can you tell which one is (ethnic nationality). He's the one carrying an Easter basket.

****

If you outlaw lutefisk, only outlaws will have lutefisk.

****

Ole went to the Doctor and the Doctor asked what was the matter. He said, "When I poke myself in the chest it hurts. When I poke myself in the arm it hurts. When I poke myself in the knee it hurts. What do you suppose is the matter?" The Doc looked at him. He said, "Well, Ole, you have a broken finger."

****

Sven and Ole always noticed that their boss always went home at four o'clock. So one day Sven said to Ole, "Why can't we do that, just one day?" So Ole and Sven took off. When Sven got home he found his boss in his wife's bedroom. He backed out and ran to Ole and said, "Ole, we must not do that again because I almost got caught."

****

Ole and Lena had an argument that ended up by Ole putting a gun to his head. His wife cried, "Don't do that, Ole!" He said, "Shut up! You're next."

****

Ole died and went to heaven where he met Lena. Ole said, "Gee, you're beautiful and this place is so beautiful. If you hadn't fed me all that oat bran, I could have been here earlier."

****

Sven asked Ole, "How are your sexual relations?" He said, "I really don't know. They didn't even come home for Thanksgiving this year."

****

Did you hear about the smart (ethnic nationality)? It's just a rumor.

****

A young carpenter asked the lumberyard salesman if he had any 2x4's. "How long do you need them?" asked the sales person. "Well," he said, "we're building a garage so I think we will need them for a long time."

****

Ole told Lena, "I'm going to go and study Hebrew at the University so that when I get to Heaven I'll be able to speak to St. Peter." Inquired Lena, "What if you go to hell?"

"Well Lena," Ole said, "I already know how to speak Norwegian."

****

Did you hear about the fellow who was so slow that it took him two hours to watch 60 Minutes.

****

Did you hear about the Scotchman that walked 18 miles to see a football game but then was too tired to climb the fence.

****

59

Scandinavians are a minority and they're smart enough to stay that way.

****

Ole was on his death bed at home. Lena was in the kitchen cooking. Ole yelled at Lena, "I smell something cooking, it really smells good, what is it?" Lena said, "It's lutefisk." Ole said, "Could you bring me some?" "No, Ole, I can't, that's for the funeral."

****

A Norwegian had a camel that would only go when he said "Uffda" and he would only stop when he said "Amen." One day he was riding his camel and was going very fast and he forgot how to get the camel to stop so he went through the entire Lord's Prayer and when he said "Amen" the camel came to an abrupt stop over a steep precipice. The Norwegian looked down, very scared and then he said "Uffda."

****

Ole received a call while having breakfast with his friends. Ole answered and then came back to the room crying. "What's the matter?" they asked. He replied, "I just got news that my mother died."

A short while later the phone rang again and Ole answered and then came back sobbing more heavily than ever. "What's the matter, now Ole?" asked his friends. "Well, it's worse than I thought, that was my brother who called, he said that his mother also died."

****

Sven had a brother in Norway. He was very proud of Ole telling all his friends that Ole was engaged in research. In fact he was so good that he was able to clone himself, but the research had one flaw. The clone Ole had a filthy mouth and embarrassed the original Ole when he went to church and attended other social functions. One day Ole decided to push his clone over one of the high cliffs or fjords on the coast of Norway. Someone saw him and they charged Ole with making an obscene clone fall.

****

A _____ called up the local auto club and wanted to know if they could send a man to open his car because he had locked himself out. The man at the office stated that he was pretty busy, but that he would be out in a couple of hours. The motorist then replied, "I hope you can make it sooner, it's starting to rain and I left the top down."

****

A _____ invented a new type of parachute. It opens on impact.

****

Do you know why _____ don't kill any flies? They are the national bird.

****

I want to tell a story. Are there any _____ in the audience? Well, in that case I'll tell it slowly.

****

I'm a _____. I can't help it. I'm taking pills for it.

****

"Do you know how to keep a _____ in suspense?"
"I'll tell you tomorrow."

****

"My birthday is on March 31."
"What year?"
"Every year."

****

An Italian immigrant with a distinct accent was bragging about his three children. "My first-a bambino, he's-a doctor. He's-a one of the best-a in his field. He make-a the $50,000 per year. My second bambino is a lawyer, and he make-a the $75,000 per year. My thirda-boy, he's-a my finest boy. He's-a sports-a mechanic."

"What," inquired my friend, "is a 'sportsamechanic'?

"He's-a person that fixes the football games, the basketball games, and all-a the other sports-a-games."

****

Three men had been sentenced to death by the guillotine in France. One was a Frenchman, one was a Englishman, and one was a German. The guillotine had not been used for some time. The first man to be strapped in was the Frenchman. The screws were loosened, but because the knife had rusted into the frame, it moved just a little bit. The rules said if the knife didn't fall, the man would go free. The second person to be strapped in was the Englishman. The same thing happened, although the knife moved down a little farther in the frame. The next was the German. And just as the executioner was ready to loosen the screws, the German looked up and said, "Hey, you would have better luck with your operation if you would put a little oil in the knife-carrying frame."

****

Recently I met a handsome man with a Nordic accent. I asked him whether he was Swedish or Norwegian. He said, "I'm Norwegian, but it's about the same."

****

There are no _____ paratroopers. The reason is that they can't count to ten.

****

EXPERTS

Like other perfectionists, I live with a constant sense of failure.

—Garrison Keillor

****

If one could cross Poison Ivy with four-leafs Clover maybe we'd have a rash of good luck.

****

The young professor had been invited to address a poultry convention. "The first thing you must do," he said, "to properly raise a flock is to separate the male chicks from the female chicks."

After he finished, a lady inquired, "Professor, how can you tell male chicks from female chicks?"

"Well," he said, "You go out into your yard and dig a pailful of worms. Then you set them before the chicks, and the male chicks will eat the male worms and the female chicks will eat the female worms."

"Yes, but, Professor, how do you tell a male worm from a female worm?"

"Madam," came the answer, "I'm a poultry expert, not a worm expert."

****

An expert is an ordinary guy 50 miles from home.

****

We have changed chairman to chairperson. Should we change fisherman to fisherperson?

****

Two men were fishing on one of the big lakes behind one of the large dams on the Missouri River in South Dakota. Accidentally, one of the men dropped his wallet over the side of the boat. Two weeks later one of the men was back fishing with another friend. All of the sudden they saw a carp jump out of the water with the wallet that had been lost two weeks previously. The carp tossed the wallet to another carp that had emerged from the water. This went on repeatedly until the last carp tossed the wallet into the boat of the fishermen. Remarked the friend, "This is the first time I've ever seen carp to carp walleting".

****

I put my fish into the freezer. He was too big to mount.

****

Work is for people who do not know how to fish.

****

The way most fishermen catch fish is by the tale.

****

A stranger approached the fisherman and said, "Are you catching any?" The fisherman replied, "Yes, about twenty." "Well," he said, "I'm the Game Warden. The limit is far less than that." Replied the fisherman, "You have just met the biggest liar you've ever met."

****

An ad in the want ad section: "WANTED - A WOMAN WHO CAN CLEAN AND COOK, DIG WORMS, SEW AND

WHO OWNS A GOOD FISHING BOAT AND MOTOR.
PLEASE ENCLOSE PHOTO OF BOAT AND MOTOR."

****

You get a line
and I'll get a pole
and we'll go fishing
on the old bass hole.

****

How does one communicate with a fish? Just drop him
a line.

****

He caught a fish so big that the negative weighed five
pounds.

****

The fish measured four inches between the eyes—via
the gullet.

****

Fisherman's Prayer:
Lord, grant that I may catch a fish
So large that even I
When speaking of it afterwards
Will have no need to lie.

****

It is impossible for Noah to have spent all his time fishing while on the Ark. Remember, he had only two worms.

****

There are two periods when fishing is good. Before you
get there and after you leave.

****

There are two kinds of fisherman—those who fish for sport and those who catch something.

****

Two fishermen were discussing last year's hunting and fishing success. The topper came when one fellow said, "I and my buddy went duck hunting. A nice flock of mallards came over this pond, and would you believe that with one single shot I got my limit of five ducks. Unfortunately, they all landed out in the middle of the pond. Not having a dog, I put on my waders and went out to get them. The water was a little deep, and spilled over into my waders. When I came back to shore with my ducks and emptied out my waders, I discovered that I also had my limit of fish."

****

FOREIGN AFFAIRS

Where is the American Embassy? Just a stones throw away from here.

****

The seven wonders of the world
were built with sweat and blood and stone,
But the wondrous thing about them all
is that they were built without a U.S. loan.

—Author Unknown

****

The way to solve the Mideast problem is to get the Jews and the Israelis to live like Christians.

****

To our Arab sheiks,

let's not be rude;
Let's remember, they're the ones
who send us crude.

****

Foreignade—the refreshment that never pauses.

****

He was tripping, not tippling, through the Orient.

****

Where's the capital of the U.S.A.? Spread all over the world.

****

FRIENDS

My wife ran off with my best friend. I sure do miss my best friend.

****

Love your friends and pray for your enemies.
—Brigham Young

****

Love God and each other. Love laughter.
—Brigham Young

****

Two can share a secret if one is dead.

****

A rumor is no good unless you repeat it.

****

If I had a ticket to heaven
And you didn't have one, too
I'd turn mine in and
Go to hell with you.

****

Some of my friends are for him and some of my friends
are against him, but I'm for my friends.

****

People who live in glass houses would make interesting
neighbors.

****

A small town is a place where if you get the wrong telephone number you'll be able to talk for fifteen minutes anyway.

****

Friends may come and go but enemies accumulate.

****

"May I have a quarter to call my friend?"
"Here's 75 cents, call all of them."

****

We should love our enemies, but we should also treat
our friends just a wee bit better.

****

I have no enemies—just a few fellows on my list in case
I change my mind.

****

I have no enemies—I've outlived most of them and I've
made friends with the others.

****

Be kind to your friends, without them you'd be a stranger.

****

A man paraphrasing a statement attributed to Mark Twain, said that if you find a hungry dog, feed him. He will not bite you and will become your best friend—and that is the main difference between man and dog.

****

They were friends until debt did them part.

****

FUND RAISING

How can you disperse a threatening mob? Start taking up a collection.

****

The armed robber pointed a gun at the proprietor and said, "Give, it will make you feel better."

****

There are fund drives for about everything under the sun. Recently I heard about one where they were raising money for the widow of the unknown soldier.

****

Peter Marshall said that life is not measured so much by one's duration as by one's donation.

****

Loving and giving
Make life worth living.

****

GAMBLING

They are putting lottery machines in the toilets. Now you can't go unless you pay.

—Jo Dean Joy

****

If ever I get even, I'll never gamble again.

****

Some people think gambling is a sin only if you lose.

****

A fellow had never flown in an airplane and he went up to the ticket counter and said, "Give me two chances to Minneapolis."

****

Las Vegas—now there's a town for my money.

****

I was lucky in Las Vegas. I got a ride home.

****

And then there was the man who went to Las Vegas in a $30,000 Cadillac and came home in a $60,000 Greyhound bus.

****

Our three-year old can count: one, two, three, four, five, six, seven, eight, nine, ten, Jack, Queen, King.

****

They have something new in Las Vegas. It's called instant bankruptcy.

****

A race horse is an animal that can take hundreds of people for a ride at the same time.

****

GOALS

"I remember," said the Floridian, "when I was up to my knees in alligators that my first objective was to drain the swamp."

****

Sportscaster: "I know that your goal was to win, but just when did the turning point come?"
Coach: "Right after they played the National Anthem."

****

You should have at least two goals in life—one to make a little money first, and secondly to make a little money last.

****

GOLF

When I drive my golf ball off the tee, I run ten yards back. This gives me a longer drive.

****

"I would move heaven and earth to get a better golf score," said the golfer to his buddy. "Better try heaven, earth you've already moved enough," replied his buddy.

****

A Sunday School teacher asked a young lad what they would turn into if they swore. "Golfers," came back the reply.

****

Did you hear about the two Scotchmen who golfed on this sweltering hot day. Mike had a stroke and Jeff counted it against his score.

****

A new golfer teed up his ball and stroke after stroke he did nothing more than dig up dirt. Finally two ants said to each other, "we better get on the ball if we are going to survive."

****

Did you hear about the golfing dentist that had eighteen cavities to fill?

****

I was playing golf the other day and I yelled "fore" and my caddie yelled back, "liar".

****

A golfer sliced five new balls into the river, so the caddie said, "Why don't you use an old one?" The golfer said, "I never owned one."

****

A golf foursome were three hours late getting back to the pro-shop. They started to complain about the twosome that were playing ahead of them and playing so slowly.

"Well," the pro informed them, "they are blind players." The first golfer then said, "Gee, I feel sorry for them. I'm going to pay for their cart." The second one said, "I'll pay for their drinks when they come in." The third one said, "I'll buy their dinner." The fourth one said, "No way am I going to do anything for them. If they were blind, why couldn't they play at night?"

****

The fat man said he didn't play golf for two reasons. For when he stood so he could hit the ball, he couldn't see it and when he stood so he could see it, he couldn't reach it.

****

A golfer sliced his shot into a bunch of trees. When he went to pick up the lost ball he found a man lying on the ground holding his forehead. The man replied, "I'm a lawyer and this is going to cost you $5,000." Whereupon the golfer replied, "I distinctly remember yelling fore." "Okay," said the lawyer, "you've got a deal."

****

Two young lads were watching a golfer as he teed off. The golfer asked, "are you watching me to learn the game?" "No," they replied, "we want to go down by the river and we need more worms."

****

Then there was a country club in the southwest years ago that would not allow Jewish people to play their golf course. Governor Janklow of South Dakota who is half Norwegian and half Jewish quipped that he would only ask to play nine holes.

****

A minister had a habit of sneaking out to the back woods golf course to play golf on Sunday afternoons. Gabriel and St. Peter, watching from above, were concerned. One day they decided that the minister should be punished. So St. Peter said to Gabriel, "I'll take care of it next Sunday." When the minister teed off the ball, it went straight down the fairway and fell into the cup. Gabriel said to St. Peter, "What kind of punishment is this?"

St. Peter replied, "Who is he going to tell?"

****

I lost only two golf balls last season—I was putting at the time.

****

There are 20 million golfers in the world and only 19,999,999 balls, and that is why, at any given moment, someone is out looking for a lost golf ball.

****

Caddy: "I'm not looking at my watch, sir, this is my compass."

****

Then there was the golfer who was so used to cheating that when he made a hole in one he wrote down zero.

****

A foursome of golfers always managed to be in by 6 p.m. One day they were a full hour late. When they came in, the pro inquired, "Whatever happened that you fellows were so late today?"

"Well," replied one, "everything was O.K. until the fourth tee, and then Frank had a stroke and died. After that it was hit the ball, drag Frank, hit the ball, drag Frank."

****

"What is your handicap?"
"My driver, my irons and my putter."

****

"This is the toughest course I've ever played on."

Caddy: "Sir, how can you tell? You haven't even been on the course yet."

****

I'm always having great difficulty deciding whether to play golf or go to church on Sunday. For example, last Sunday I had to flip a coin 27 times.

****

Golf is really a stupid game. I'm glad I don't have to play it again until next week.

****

"Reverend, is it a sin to play golf on Sunday?"

"In your case, it's a sin every day."

****

A lot of ministers don't play golf because they don't have the vocabulary for it.

****

"How's your daughter's golf?"

"Oh, she's going around in less and less every day."

"Yes, I know, but how's her golf?"

****

GOOD NEWS — BAD NEWS

Custer had a scout named LeRoy. He came back after a scouting mission and informed the general that he had good news and bad news. "What's the good news, LeRoy," inquired the general. "We're surrounded," replied LeRoy. "Good," replied the general. "We don't have to go back to Bismarck."

****

Did you hear about the fella that fell out of the apple tree and broke a limb?

****

My friend arranged a blind date for me, so I got a new pair of bib overalls and went to the party. I approached the young lady and asked her, "Are you Elaine?" "Yes," she said. Then she asked, "Are you Al?" I said, "Yes". Then she said, "Then I'm not Elaine."

****

A pilot flying a superjet for the first time turned on the intercom in the cockpit and told his passengers that he had both good news and bad news for them. The good news was that they were making real good time, and the bad news was that they were lost.

****

A man was telling his friend how his airplane engine had failed.
"That's bad," replied his friend.
"No, I had a parachute."
"That was good."
"No, it didn't open."
"That was bad."
"No, there was a haystack below."
"That was good."
"No, there was a pitchfork in the haystack."
"That was bad."
"No, I missed it."

****

A fellow jumped out of the top window of a skyscraper. As he was passing a window half way down, he was overheard to remark, "So far, so good."

****

Which is worse? Population explosion or government explosion?

****

The seven wonders of the world
were built with sweat and blood and stone
but the wondrous thing about them all is
that they were built without a USA loan

****

Our forefathers wanted representative government in the worst way. Their hopes have been fulfilled. Just watch Congress in action.

****

Bismarck supposedly said, "Never watch how sausages and laws are made."

****

Show me a man with his problems behind him and I'll show you the President's chauffeur.

****

The editor of a small weekly newspaper had a headline that read "Half the City Officials are Crooks". The city fathers descended on his office and demanded a retraction. He said, "OK, gentlemen, I will retract it in my next edition." When that edition came out it's headline read "Half the City Officials are not Crooks".

****

Our mayor is the finest that money can buy.

****

George Washington was the only President who didn't blame the previous administration for all of his problems.

****

FDR on a political campaign trail stated that he was a friend of labor, a friend of industry, but when he had a really big problem, he takes it to a higher authority. A member of the audience replied, "and I don't like her either."

****

In our country, one can say what he thinks and if he doesn't think he can still say it.

****

Too bad our grandchildren can't be around to see all the wonderful things we're doing with their money.

****

Blessed are the young, for they shall inherit the national debt.

****

Only Americans have fostered the art of being prosperous, though broke.

****

I'm disturbed by laws designed to prohibit winners from being winners in order to prevent losers from being losers.

****

Whenever one man gets something without earning it, some other man has to earn something without getting it.

****

If you think OSHA is a small town in Wisconsin you have another think coming.

****

God gives every bird his food, but he doesn't throw it into the nest.

****

A young orphan boy who was having some difficult times wrote a letter addressed to God. "Dear God," he said, "I would really appreciate it if you could send me $100 so that my sisters and I can have better food and some clothing." He signed it and sent it to Washington D.C.

Several months later a letter postmarked Washington arrived with a five dollar bill in it. The little boy sat down and wrote another letter.

"Dear God, thanks so much for the $5. But if you don't mind, next time please don't send it through Washington — they deducted $95 for administrative costs."

****

GROWING OLDER AND RETIREMENT

The stages of life may be described as follows. Youth looks ahead.

Old age looks backward. Middle age looks worried.

****

"How many years of life do you think you have left?" I asked my eighty-eight year old friend. He replied, "At my age I'm not even buying green bananas anymore."

—Shepersky

****

How old am I? Well, when I try to blow out the candles on my birthday cake, the heat drives me back.

****

79

The worst thing about growing old is that you have to listen to your children's advice.

****

I'm at the stage of life where the happy hour is a nap.

****

I'm somewhere between sin and Sun City.

****

Four signs of getting old:
1. You forget faces.
2. You forget names.
3. You forget to zip up.
4. You forget to zip down.

****

Two old men were chatting. Inquired the first, "I can't remember your name." Replied the second, "How soon do you have to know?"

****

The only problem with being retired is that you are on the job when you wake up.

****

Before you decide to retire, stay home and watch some of the daytime TV programs.

****

An 80 year old lady in a retirement home was admiring a ninety year old man. "Why do you keep looking at me so much?" inquired the old man. "Well," she said, "you look just like my third husband." "How many husbands have you had?" he asked. "Two," she replied.

****

"I miss the old spittoon," said the husband. "You always did," replied his wife.

****

Of all the things that I have lost in my lifetime, I miss the loss of my memory the most.

****

Burning the candle on each end
doesn't bother me a bit.
The problem at my age
is to keep both ends lit.

****

Age is a quality of mind.
For if your dreams you've left behind
and hope is cold,
And you no longer look ahead
and life's ambitions fires are dead,
then you are old.
But if in life you seek the best,
If in life you keep the zest,
If love you hold,
then no matter how the Birthdays fly,
then you're not old.

—Anonymous

****

I'm not as old as I look. I married young. I worried a lot and molted prematurely.

****

Old actors and actresses never die. They just fade away and do commercials.

****

When I grow old I'll be sedate
I'll go to bed each night at eight
But while I'm young, I'll have some fun
At least until I'm ninety-one.

****

Middle age men are easy to spot
On the top they are thinning
In the middle, they're not.

****

There are three stages to men: youth, middle age and "you're looking good."

****

A ninety year-old man was asked his formula for such a long life and he replied, "Just keep breathing."

****

Art Linklatter On Old Age ...
"My grandfather got married at 92."
"Why would anyone wait to get married until so old?"
"He had to."

"You're old if you sit in a rocking chair and can't get it started."

"You're old when you feel like the morning after and you hadn't been out the night before."

"You're getting old if your back goes out more often than you do."

****

You're getting old when the number of things you can no longer do is roughly equal to the number of things you no longer want to do.

****

After the age of 65 what doesn't hurt, doesn't work.

****

You can add years to your life simply by telling the truth about your age.

****

The older I get, the better I used to be.

—Lee Trevino

****

Al's friend who hadn't seen him for a long time greeted him by stating, "My you're looking good, Al, but then I do remember when you were good looking."

****

An elderly man ordered a martini at the bar and said to the waiter, "Please put a prune in my martini."

****

Many ills are cured by telling the sick person that the symptoms of his illness are signs of advancing age.

****

After age 40 you become nothing more than a maintenance problem.

****

Grandma no longer wears her nightcap—she drinks it.

****

There are three things that happen to you when you grow older. First you begin to lose your eyesight, then you tend to forget, and third—I can't remember.

****

There are three stages to man—the first 20 years he learns, the next 20 he earns, and the next 20 he yearns.

****

A patient came to see his doctor and said, "I think I'm losing my memory."

"How long has this been going on?" inquired the doctor.

"How long has what been going on?" asked the patient.

****

Three elderly gentlemen were talking. One said, "I remember Teddy Roosevelt."

The second said, "I remember Woodrow Wilson."

And the third said, "I remember Elizabeth Taylor."

"Well," responded one of the guys, "she's not even dead yet."

"Neither am I," said the speaker.

****

When you no longer need a pillow to play Santa Claus, you're middle aged.

****

You're not old when your teeth decay,
You're not old when your hair turns gray,
But you're old as sure as the sea is deep
If your head makes dates that your feet can't keep.

****

Well, there's one thing to be said in favor of being over 40. Women are still interested in you, but the army isn't.

****

Though I'll soon be pushing 60
I'm as solid as a rock,
And a devil at all parties
At least until nine o'clock.

****

My first 75 years have taught me that if you stick around long enough you'll see everything—twice.

—Quincy Howe

****

HIPPIES AND YUPPIES

A guy with a mane in Spain stays mostly on the plane.

****

A hippie walking down the street with one shoe was asked, "Did you lose a shoe?"

"No," came back the reply, "I found one."

****

The very first rock festival was staged by David and Goliath.

****

There's one thing to be said for long hair and beards. They're a boon to people with ugly faces.

****

At the wedding ceremony, the minister said, "Will one or the other of you please give the ring to the bride?"

****

A man and his wife argued about whether four hippies that they were observing were girls. The lady finally approached the group and asked, "Are you sisters?"

"No," one of them responded, "we're not even Catholic."

****

I have an amazing memory for events that never happened.

****

Did you ever think that the far east would ultimately be so near?

****

READER'S NOTE: General Custer was considered one of this nation's great post-Civil War army generals. His defeat and the total annihilation of his troops at the Battle of the Little Big Horn have precipitated dozens of Custer stories. Here are a few examples:
Custer's last words: "Where in H— did all these Indians come from?"

****

General Custer was a well-dressed man. When they found him he was wearing an Arrow shirt.

****

Many communities in eastern Dakota fail to grow and prosper because when Custer went through there he told the citizens, "Don't do anything until I return."

****

As General Custer fell mortally wounded, he cried out to the soldiers, "Take no prisoners."
So much for the Custer stories—

****

If our first president, George Washington, was first in war, first in peace, and first in the hearts of his countrymen, why is it that he married a widow?

****

History repeats itself because we didn't listen the first time.

****

If it were not for Thomas Edison we would be watching television by candlelight.

****

Abraham Lincoln was once taken to task by an associate for his attitude toward his enemies.

"Why," he was asked, "do you try to make friends with them? You should try to destroy them."

To which Lincoln replied, "Am I not destroying my enemies when I make them my friends?"

****

HOMETOWN

The town was too small for a full-time drunk so they took turns.

****

My town is so small that the only thing we do for excitement is to go over to the depot on Saturdays to see the train come in.

****

A small town is a place where everyone knows whose check is good and whose husband isn't.

****

I refuse to fly in anything bigger than my hometown. When that 747 took off I thought the whole airport was taking off.

****

I come from a town that has 400 souls—and about the same number of heels.

****

It's a wonderful town. When I arrived I couldn't speak, I couldn't walk, I scarcely had any hair on my head, and they had to lift me from my bed. I was born here.

****

Our town was so small that the last one home at night turned out the street lights.

****

Not much to see, but what you hear makes up for it.

****

Ours is a friendly city. If you will check the yellow pages in our phone book you will find that we have more doctors ushering in the newborn than we have undertakers ushering out the dead.

****

HUNTING

Paul took his friend, Rich, turkey hunting in the beautiful Black Hills of South Dakota. A game warden supervising the turkey hunting season had informed all hunters that in case they got lost which happens frequently, the hunter was to fire three shots into the air and to remain in that area until the game warden found them.

Sure enough, Paul and Rich got lost. It being late in the afternoon, Paul said to Rich, "you better fire those three shots."

Rich did as he was told and waited and waited and nobody came. As it was getting dark, Paul said, "Rich, you better fire another three shots." Rich replied, "Paul, you better fire yours because I'm out of arrows."

****

Flocks of geese always fly in a vee formation. One line is usually longer than the other. Why is this so? Answer: One line has more geese in it than the other.

****

The duck hunter was telling his friends that he was so good with his new duck call that the previous morning he was able to raise three decoys.

****

Two men hunting bear in Alaska camped out in the woods. Early one morning one of the men went out to the restroom some distance from the hunting shack. He yelled to his buddy that a bear was heading their way. As the bear was closing in on the first hunter, the one noticed that his buddy was putting on a pair of tennis shoes. He yelled to him, "you don't have time to put on those shoes. You can't outrun him!" Replied the second hunter, "I don't intend to outrun him, just you!"

****

He gave his hunting dog some Valium so instead of pointing when he spotted the bird, he just waved his tail.

****

He doesn't hunt elephants. He claims the decoys are too heavy to carry.

****

Why does a duck walk softly? It's because it can't walk hardly.

****

The game warden said to the farmer, "It is reported that you shot a Loon. Loon's are an endangered species." "I didn't know that," said the farmer, "but I can tell you that they taste better than Bald Eagles or Whooping Cranes."

****

A hunter lost in the wilds of northern Minnesota screamed at his guide, "You told me you were the best guide in Minnesota."

"Yes," replied the guide, "I am, but I think we're in Canada now."

****

Two fellows went duck hunting. One told his new-found friend that he was known to snore at night, and if he did hear him snoring, to simply get up and shake him. Shortly after they turned out the lights, his buddy went over to his bunk and kissed him on the cheek. There was no snoring that night.

****

An old hunter preparing his own shells rammed in a charge of salt. "Why," asked his hunting buddy, "are you doing that?"

"Well," he said, "when I drop those bucks way out, it keeps the meat from spoiling until I get there."

They call it take home pay because there's no other place you can afford to go with it.

****

A man said that his biggest financial problem was at the end of the month when he had too much month left and not enough money.

****

"Give me twenty cents worth of potatoes."
"Why don't you take a whole one?"

****

If you want to teach a child the value of a dollar, you'd better do it quickly.

****

If you think the cost of living is high, just wait until your wife gets your funeral bill.

****

Inflation is now so bad that it takes three to make a pair.

****

It costs more to live today, but I wonder if it is worth more.

****

It's tough to pay $5.00 for a steak, but it's tougher if you pay $1.50.

****

If your neighbor sued you because your fence encroached on his property should you be advised to get a defense lawyer?

****

A man called his lawyer and said, "I just shot a man and I'll give you fifty thousand dollars to defend me in court." Lawyer: "I'll be right over and I'll bring three witnesses to testify that you didn't do it."

****

We have nearly a million lawyers in the United States compared to about twenty thousand in Japan. As much as Japan has a surplus of Hondas and we apparently a surplus of lawyers, someone came up with the idea that we trade Hondas for lawyers. The Japanese considered it, but decided against it for the simple reason they concluded that there would be too much "suishi" and "suihi."

****

The Mennonite Bible states that if a brother offends another brother he should go and see him to resolve the matter. If not able to settle it, they are to get two elders and have the case settled by them. A brother duo could not resolve a case so they went to see the elders. One elder listened to first brother and stated that he made a very convincing case and that he was right. Then the second elder listened to the other and said, "You also made a very convincing case and you are right also." The second elder then grabbed the first elder and said, "Both cannot be right." The first elder replied, "And you are right, too."

—Reuben Goertz

****

Three fellows were found murdered in the back alley in Chicago. Each had a box of Grape-Nuts under their arms. The detective visiting the murder scene declared, "It undoubtedly is a serial killer." A bystander was asked what she saw. She replied, "Nut 'n' honey."

****

Support your local lawyer, send your kids to medical school.

****

It was so cold that I saw a lawyer with his hands in his own pocket.

****

I went to our company library to check out a book on ethics, but found out that the book had been stolen.

****

"There once was a young lawyer man
Who gently smiled as he began
Her dear dead husband's will to scan.
And thinking of his coming fee
He said to her quite tenderly
You have a nice fat legacy.
Next morning as he lay in bed
With bandages on his smashed-in head
He wondered what in the heck he said.

—Anonymous

****

"Daddy, slow down. The policeman on the motorcycle can't get by you."

****

Where there is a will, there is a lawyer.

****

A real law abiding citizen is one that gets a parking ticket and rejoices in the fact that the system works.

****

The defense lawyer obtained a suspended sentence for his client. They hung him.

****

A truck carrying a load of toupees tipped over and the police ended up combing the entire area.

****

A patrol office saw this big rig going down the highway at 80 miles an hour, so the patrol officer called the trucker on his CB. "Hey trucker, how fast are you going?" The trucker replied, "Just 55 miles an hour officer." "Well," said the patrol officer, "better brace yourself, your trailer is going at 80 miles an hour."

****

Times have changed, friends used to say when they left, "I'll be seeing you." Now frequently they'll say, "I'll be suing you."

****

What do you call a mobster embedded in cement? A hardened criminal.

****

Judge: "You were brought in here for drinking."
Defendant: "When do we start, Your Honor?"

****

"Why didn't you try to settle the case out of court?" the judge asked the litigants.
"That's just what we were trying to do when the police came and interfered."

****

If the law is on my side, I hammer on the law.

If the facts are on my side, I hammer on the facts.

If neither the law nor the facts are on my side, I hammer on the table.

****

"I'll give you 30 days or $100," said the judge.

"I'll take the $100," replied the defendant.

****

Only lawyers can write documents containing 5,000 or more words and call it a brief.

****

LIARS

Liar's Club Nominations

It was late in the fall and I saw this fine flock of Mallard ducks land into a fast freezing pond of water. I watched them for a while, then took aim thinking that I would get my limit in one shot. The entire flock flapped their wings and took off carrying a big sheet of ice with them. The ice melted over Nebraska City, Nebraska and flooded the entire town.

****

When I was in Riyad, Saudia Arabia in 1976, it was so hot that when the waitress put a cube of ice into my water it melted so fast that it left a hole in it.

****

My love for her is greater than the national debt.

****

The first time my wife and I went to the movies we held hands. She held hers and I held mine.

****

He came from such a large family that he didn't sleep alone until he was married.

****

I came home and saw my wife scrubbing the floor so I asked her, "Are you off your rocker?"

****

A man who claims he is boss in his own home will lie about other things also.

****

"Congratulations," said the caller, "on your fiftieth anniversary. It sounds so exciting." The husband replied, "Not as exciting as it was fifty years ago."

****

Talk about being cheap. My friend is so cheap that he went on his honeymoon alone.

****

Eve asked Adam, "Do you really love me?" Adam replied, "Who else?"

****

Bob Hope was asked on his and Delores' sixtieth wedding anniversary why they stayed together so long. He replied, "It's because of the kids. We're waiting for them to die."

****

How long have you been married? "I don't rightly know, but I can tell you that we are on our second bottle of Tabasco sauce."

****

Two women were talking about their husbands. Said the one, "The things I admired most about my husband were his appearance, his brains, his health and his wealth." The other replied, "I like all those things, but the appearance most of all and the sooner the better."

****

Said the wife to the husband, "Doesn't that lady look terrible with that low cut gown." Replied the husband, "Not so far as I can see."

****

"If on the street
You catch me staring
I'm not flirting
I'm comparing."

****

Courtship is that period during which a girl decides whether or not she can do better.

****

A neighbor told his neighbor that he ought to pull his shades at night because last night he saw him kissing his wife. "Ho, Ho," replied the neighbor, "Jokes on you, I wasn't home last night."

****

Did you hear about the Scotchman who took his pregnant wife out on his country mail route so that he would receive a rural free delivery?

****

A young lady told her mother: "All I'm looking for is a man who's kind and understanding. Mother, is that too much to expect of a millionaire?"

****

Ole and Lena sat rocking on the front porch. Ole dozed off. Lena slapped him and Ole asked why. Said she, "For being such a poor lover." After awhile Lena dozed off and Ole slapped her and Lena asked, "Why did you slap me?" Replied Ole, "For knowing the difference."

****

An elderly widow lady was walking on the beach in Miami when she met a man who stopped to talk to her. "You don't have a tan," she said to him, "where are you from?" "New York," replied the man. "I just got out of prison after spending 24 years there."

"What for?" inquired the lady.

"Murdering my wife," came the man's reply. "Oh," she said, "then you must be single."

****

Two wives are bigamy and one wife is monotony.

****

"How do you know that you're happily married?"
"Our counselor told us so."

****

Henry VIII said to his last wife, "I shan't keep you long."

****

There was a couple who had a water bed. He named it Lake Placid.

****

An Irishman was asked whether he was well off when he got married. "Yes," he said, "I was, but I didn't know it."

****

Lena said to Ole, "I'm going to have a baby." Ole responded, "With you being Norwegian and I being Norwegian, I'm sure the baby will be 100 percent Norwegian." "No dear," said Lena, "it's going to be Cesarean."

****

Often you can surprise your spouse on his or her birthday just by mentioning it.

****

Married men have better halves, bachelors have better quarters.

****

"How did you make out in that fight with your wife?"
"Just fine, she came crawling to me on her hands and knees, and said come out from under that bed, you coward."

****

"Who gave you that black eye?"
"My wife."
"I thought she was out of town."
"So did I."

****

You're nobody until somebody loves you and the next thing you know you are a den mother.

****

After a noisy argument, a wife snapped at her husband, "Did you hear my last remark?"

"I certainly hope so," he replied.

****

Most women could be cured of jealousy if they'd just take one good impartial look at their husbands.

****

Let her stay home and wash and iron and cook and clean and take care of the kids. No wife of mine is going to work.

****

A man complained about having had two unhappy marriages. His first wife divorced him and his second one wouldn't.

****

A second marriage is a triumph of hope over experience.

****

He is not chasing women any more. First of all, he's lost his interest, second his inclination, and third, his wind.

****

The guy that said that talk is cheap probably never said, "I do."

****

"I've been married for thirty years, and it hasn't been half bad."

"How so?"

"I've been gone half the time."

****

My wife and I have had a very simple relationship down through the years. I rule the roost and she rules the rooster.

****

I proposed to my wife in the garage and couldn't back out.

****

Marriage is a wonderful thing. It's the living together afterwards that causes all of the difficulties.

****

Dear, don't expect the first few meals to be very good. It takes time to find the right restaurants.

****

A running mate is a husband who dared to talk back.

****

The biggest cause of divorce is marriage.

****

I married for better or for worse—she couldn't do any worse and I couldn't do any better.

****

"Why did you get married?"
"What else was there to do?"

****

I try to argue with my wife but every time I do words fail me.

****

A gentleman was found sitting on the steps of the county courthouse on a Monday morning. When an employee arrived, he inquired of the gentleman why he was there so early. He answered, "I've just come to see when my marriage license expires."

****

MATHEMATICS

A Missouri farmer passed away and left seventeen mules to his three sons. The instructions left in the will said that the oldest boy was to get 1/2, the second eldest 1/3, and the youngest 1/9. The three sons, recognizing the difficulty of dividing seventeen mules into these fractions, began to argue. The uncle heard about the argument, hitched up his mule and drove out to settle the matter. He added his mule to the 17, making it 18. The eldest son therefore got 1/2 or nine; the second got 1/3 or six; and the youngest got 1/9 or two. Adding up 9, 6, and 2 equals 17. The uncle, having settled the argument, hitched up his mule and drove home.

****

Dad, I can explain the poor grade I got in math. The batteries in my calculator went dead.

****

MEDICINE, HEALTH AND PSYCHIATRY

A person feeling somewhat distressed called a psychiatrist and asked what he could do for him for fifty dollars. Replied the psychiatrist, "I will send you a get well card."

****

You can live a long time if you can learn how to take care of a chronic disease.

—Steve Schock

****

Did you know that fifty percent of all professionals graduated at the bottom of their class. This includes doctors.

****

A man met a friend coming out of a psychiatrist office. "Are you coming or going?" he inquired. His friend replied, "If I knew which I wouldn't be here."

****

A doctor fell into the well
And broke his collarbone
I think that the doctors ought to tend the sick
And leave the well alone.

****

The pharmaceutical company announced that it had a new miracle drug that could save the lives of thousands, but it would take the FDA ten years to grant approval because they want to determine it's side effects - like five hundred thousand dead.

****

The patient said to the Doctor, "I'm so worried because I can't even remember the street I live on." Replied the Doc, "don't worry, it may just be a mental block."

****

The wife said to the nurse, "I'm going to leave my husband here until he is well healed." Replied the nurse, "The only ones that leave here well-heeled are the doctors."

****

Inquired the patient of his doctor, "What is it this time? Something that I have to live with or something I have to live without."

****

I read recently that not laughing at another's jokes may cause cancer.

****

"Does the Doctor you married have any money?" asked the father. "Of course, Dad. Did you think I got married for my health."

****

A 46 year-old lady went to see a psychiatrist. He asked why a 46 year-old lady married a 75 year-old man. She replied, "I thought he was 85."

****

Did you hear about the podiatrist who decided to become a detective and found something loose of foot?

****

I'll never go to a doctor whose office plants have died.
—Erma Bombeck

****

Brother Ozzie said he gets enough exercise by being one of the pallbearers for his jogging friends.

****

A neurotic person builds castles in the sky. A psychotic person lives in those castles. A psychiatrist collects rent from both.

****

One of every five people has a mental problem. If the four seated near you look normal, then you're the one with the problem.

****

The best exercise for the heart is to reach down and lift someone up.

****

They gave me so much penicillin for my cold that if I sneeze, I'll cure most of you in the front row.

****

If drinking is so bad, why are there more old drunks than old doctors.

****

I'm tired this morning. I was breathing all night.

****

"Are you troubled by improper thoughts?"
"No, I rather enjoy them."

****

The man told his psychiatrist that he had a real problem. One night he would dream that he was in a tepee and the next night he would dream that he was in a wigwam. Then it would repeat, on and on. The doctor said, "I don't think it's anything serious, you just have to relax. You are too tents."

****

If you are strong enough to do fifty pushups a day then you probably don't need to exercise.

****

A laboring man showed one morning all dressed up in his Sunday best. His fellow employee said, "What's up today, Herb? Why are you all dressed up?"

"Well," he said, "I'm going to the doctor to have a vasectomy." "Why is that so important to dress up for?"

"Well," he said, "when you're going to be impotent, you should dress like your important."

****

Humor, a good sense of it, is to Americans what manhood is to Spaniards and we will go to great lengths to prove it. Experiments with laboratory rats have shown that if one psychologist in the room laughs at something a rat does, all the other psychologists will laugh equally. Nobody wants to be left holding a joke.

—Garrison Keillor

****

I won't eat organic food. At my age I need all the preservatives that I can get.

****

Did you ever notice that most of the clerks in health food stores look like death warmed over.

****

A practical nurse is one who marries a rich patient.

****

Addressing his medical students, the professor noted the muscle of the patient's leg had contracted until it was much shorter than the other, thus he limps. Now he asked the class, "What would you do in such a circumstance?" Replied one of the students, "I would limp too."

****

Two young ladies went shopping. When they parked they found a dead cat on the street. They put it into a shopping bag and placed it on top of the car thinking that they would dispose of it when they returned. An elderly lady saw this shopping bag on top of the car, kept looking around and then pushed it into her own shopping bag. The two young ladies went into the restaurant to eat when the elderly lady came into the restaurant and sat down beside them. The elderly lady's curiosity got the best of her so she peeked into the bag which she had just shoplifted off the car and low and behold there she saw the dead cat. She immediately fainted. The restaurant operator called the ambulance, they came in with a stretcher, put the lady on the stretcher and placed the shopping bag with the dead cat on top of her. One can only wonder what the reaction of the doctors and nurses was when the lady arrived in the emergency room at the hospital.

****

"How did you become president of your company?"
"Well, I attribute it all to the physical fitness program that our company conducted. Every time one of our jogging friends dropped over with a heart attack, I moved up another notch."

****

There was a chiropractor that said that the backbone served three main functions. First, to support the head. Secondly to support the rib cage and thirdly to support the chiropractors.

****

When you go to see a chiropractor, be prepared to receive a lot of back talk.

****

I feel like a Snapdragon. I have no snap and everything is dragging.

****

Do you pay the doctor that does acupuncture with pin money?

****

If you don't have charity in your heart, you have the worst type of heart trouble.

—Brian Mortenson

****

I won't eat natural foods. I just read that 90 percent of all people die of natural causes.

****

The hospital service was so poor that when they called 911 from the Emergency Room no one came.

****

Coming out of his operation the patient asked, "Doctor, was the operation successful?"

"I can't say, I'm not your doctor, I'm Saint Peter."

****

We have a doctor in our town that has so much charm and personality that when he takes a woman's pulse, he automatically subtracts 10 points for his own personality.

****

A lady called her doctor in the middle of the night inquiring how much he charged for a house call and how much for an office call. The doctor told her that a house call was $25 and an office call was $15.

She then replied, "I'll see you in your office in about thirty minutes."

****

A man went to the hospital to get a cardiogram. After the cardiogram had been taken, he was given a sheet of paper with a whole bunch of jiggly lines on it. He took it home and put it into his player piano and it played back, "Nearer My God to Thee."

****

He went to Phoenix for his sinus—finally got it after ten years.

****

A well-adjusted person is one whose intake of pep pills just overbalances his intake of tranquilizers, leaving enough energy for his weekly trip to the psychiatrist.

****

You've got another one of those nasty colds. It's too bad you don't have pneumonia, we know how to cure that.

****

"Cheer up," said the doctor, "I've had the same thing myself."
"But you didn't have the same doctor," replied the patient.

****

An ulcer is a pain in the neck that has localized itself in the stomach.

****

You get ulcers not from what you eat, but from what's eating you.

****

Virus is a Latin word used by doctors to mean, "Your guess is as good as mine."

****

"Doctor, if the pain in my right leg is caused by old age, why doesn't my left leg hurt—it's the same age."

****

A patient who had been informed that his illness was terminal joined the Communist Party. When asked why, he replied, "It's better that one of them should go."

****

Please sit down before someone less desirable sits next to me.

****

Greeting by a Southern governor to a convention group: You all have a good time. You all be careful now, you hear?

****

Many a man goes to a convention in a state of confusion, returns the same way, but, we trust, on a higher level.

****

Meetings and conventions are functions which one attends to learn things he already knows, but which he does not have time to put in practice because there are so many meetings and conventions to attend.

****

A meeting is a collection of individuals who individually can do nothing, but who get together and collectively decide that nothing can be done.

****

Taking your wife to a convention is like taking the game warden on a hunting trip.

****

MEMBERSHIP DRIVES

I never join an organization willing to have me.
—Tom Killian

****

We had a membership drive last week and drove out ten members.

****

The Communist Party in Russia had a membership drive. The rules were as follows: Any Communist who could recruit a new member would no longer have to pay dues. If he got two members, he would be permitted to leave the party, and if he recruited three members he would receive a certificate stating that he had never belonged in the first place.

****

Once I had joined the organization and paid my dues, I inquired as to what my privileges were. Back came the answer, "You can pay dues again next year."

****

MEN

We talked about all the important people in our city this morning -but your name never came up.

****

My wife asked me to pull in my stomach, but I already had.

****

It never occurs to a young man that some day he will be as dumb as his father.

****

A bigamist is a man who keeps two himself.

****

The father said to the son, "At your age Lincoln was up every night studying." "Yes, Dad, but at your age, he was also President."

****

A Londoner had invited an English countryman from the English hinterlands to join him at the Men's Club in downtown London.

After being seated in the lounge the Londoner inquired of his friend, "Can I offer you a drink?" "No," he said. "I don't drink. I tried it once and didn't like it." Then the Londoner said, "Could I offer you a cigar?" "No, thank you," he said, "I tried it once and didn't like it. But I have a son, and I'll take it home for him." Where upon the Londoner said, "And I suppose, an only son."

****

He's got all the men in his company standing on their toes. He has raised all the urinals in the men's room.

****

"You asked me that my youth is spent
While my get up and go has gone and went
But, boy, how I grin
When I think where it's been."

—Jack Stickly

****

He is an elderly wolf. He won't lust much longer.

****

The wind that blows the skirts so high
Has a fiendish, gutsy glee
Of blowing dust into the eyes
Of he who turns to see.

****

A more Biblical version of the foregoing:

The naughty East wind comes and blows
The maiden's skirt on high
But heaven is just and sends the dust
To blind the bad man's eye.

****

A wolf whose wink has been returned
May be on the verge of being burned.

****

I asked my wife how many great men there were in the world. She replied, "one less than you think."

****

Middle age men are easy to spot
On the top they are thinning
In the middle, they're not.

****

There are three stages to men: youth, middle age and "you're looking good".

****

He's real good to his wife, he never goes home.

****

Definition for menopause. Change of wife.

****

When it comes to charity many men will stop at nothing.

****

The mountaineer said, "Do come into my boar's nest, I do clean it every thirty days, but I'm already ninety days behind."

****

The average woman soon discovers that her ideal man isn't real and her real man isn't ideal.

****

When men get too old to set bad examples, they sit around dishing out good advice.

****

Before he was married, he had three theories on children—now he has three children and no more theories.

****

The modern man is a person who drives a mortgaged car on a bond-financed highway with gas purchased on a credit card.

****

She's my type — a woman.

****

MILITARY

A sergeant addressing his platoon said, "we don't want any 'yes' men around in this outfit, agreed?"

****

The war was going bad for Japan so they began to recruit young kamikaze pilots from the hinterland of Japan. Gathering a number of then together, the commanding officer explained exactly what their duties would be. When you see that American ship out there in the Pacific you hone right in on it and crash your plane and yourself into it. Are there any questions? From the back of the room, a young recruit raised his hand. "Yes," he said, "Officer, are you out of your cotton picking mind?"

****

Did you hear about the person who raised funds for widow of the Unknown Soldier?

****

Said a World War II veteran, "I'll always be grateful for that French lassie that hid me in the basement of her parents home - for three months."

****

If your parachute doesn't open up for you, you've obviously jumped to a conclusion.

****

Is it true that all generals have aides?

****

Faster, faster
pushed on our way
Crowding a lifetime
into a day
Spun across continents
hurtled through space
No wonder we are called
the human race.

****

The next war will be fought in outer space
And who could think of a better place.

****

The base commander of the army post stopped a young recruit for failing to salute. "Do you know who I am?" he inquired of the recruit. "I'm the commander of this base of twenty-five thousand."

"Sir," replied the recruit, "I really don't know who you are, but if you have that many men under your care, you better be careful not to louse up."

****

Ready on the Right
Ready on the Left
Fire at will!
New recruit: Who is Will?

****

Nervous recruit on guard duty: "Who went there?"

****

A Vietnam veteran was asked how he got the Purple Heart. He said, "I was on the front line and I yelled to the Vietnamese enemy, 'To hell with Ho Chi Men'." He yelled back, "To hell with LBJ." Both of us got out of our fox holes, shook hands, and got run over by a tank."

****

A new recruit was asked why he joined the army. He said there were three reasons. First, he wanted to serve his country. Second, he wanted to build himself up physically. Third, they came and got him.

****

Recently I heard a suggestion that the way to cut the defense budget was to reduce the Pentagon to a triangle.

****

An enlisted man was called into the military court for having called a Lieutenant a SOB. The chaplin was asked to defend him. The chaplin began, "Did you point a finger at the Lieutenant and call him a SOB?"

"No," replied the defendant. "Did you call the Lieutenant by name and call him a SOB?"

"No," replied the defendant. "Why would anyone accuse you of calling the Lieutenant a SOB?" "Only because everyone knew he was the only SOB around."

****

Churchill on returning from the front lines in the Boer War: "There's nothing quite so exhilarating as being shot at without result."

****

I once new an admiral by the name of Tuna. He was called "Chicken of the Sea."

****

Why not let women fight in combat? Why let all those years of marriage go to waste.

****

A time frame: Christmas before the coalition forces pushed Sadam Hussein back out of Kuwait.
"Twas the night before Christmas when all through my brain,
Nothing was stirring except Sadam Hussein.
Then I thought of a plan to knock Iraq prone,
Just open in Baghdad a savings and loan."

****

There was a soldier who got a gold medal for bravery. He was so proud of it that he had it bronzed.

****

Once I knew a mean Army officer who was rotten to the corps.

****

"I suppose after I get discharged," said the tough old squad sergeant, "you'll all be waiting in line to spit on my grave."

"No, sir, sarge," replied one of the privates, "once I'm out of the Army, I'll never stand in line again."

****

The draft board has classified me 5-F. I will be sent overseas in case our country is invaded.

****

Near the end of World War II, an army general came to review the troops in western Europe. Two privates had been positioned to open the door of the car. As the general alighted from the front seat, the first private stepped up and kicked him in the pants. The second private, standing near the rear door, took one step forward and also kicked the general.

This episode results in a court martial hearing. When the first private was asked why he had kicked the general, he said he really didn't know, that it was just an impulsive thing.

They then asked the second private his reason. "Well, sir," he responded, "when I saw my buddy kick the general, I thought the war was over."

****

If you think old soldiers fade away, you ought to see my husband trying to get into his old uniform.

****

The young recruit was going through the process of having a physical examination. When the doctor had completed the examination, he said, "Do you see that bottle on the shelf over there? I'm going to need a specimen."

"From here?" shot back the recruit.

****

My son must have a lot of untidy officers in his regiment. He's always writing about having to clean up the officers' mess.

****

The way to increase our military strength abroad tenfold is to bring home our soldiers and arm our tourists.

****

The Russians have a new submarine. It can surface and resubmerge in 22 seconds. We sure must take our hats off to the Russians, especially those left standing on the deck.

****

MONEY

Did you hear about the rich guy that bought a limousine but had nothing to chauffeur it?

****

I was robbed. They stole all of my silver — two quarters and a dime.

****

The one thing rich people have in common is - money.

****

Money isn't everything. There are such other things as stocks, CD's, bonds, traveler's checks, letters of credit, etc.

****

I should like to open a joint bank account - with someone that has money.

****

"I wish I had enough money to buy an elephant," the young man said. "What in the world would you do with an elephant?"

"Nothing," he said, "I just need the money."

****

My friend, Al Neuharth, who founded *USA Today* and became very wealthy said that the morning he left for Sioux Falls, South Dakota for a special recognition banquet, he had to check his wallet as extra baggage.

****

Money won't make you happy, it will just keep you comfortable while you're unhappy.

****

I'm very proud of the fact that I've never been overdrawn at my bank — just underdeposited.

****

Rich or poor, it's always nice to have money.

****

If you count all of your assets, you will always show a profit.

****

A loan officer in the bank told the president, "I've never made a bad loan. Of course," he said, "some went bad."

****

The Grand Canyon was created by a Scotchman who dropped a nickel into a gopher hole.

****

Money is not important. Henry Ford had millions and never owned a Cadillac.

****

The two dollar bills make buck-passing twice as difficult.

****

I sure can't describe pornography, but I sure as heck can tell it when I see it.

* * * * * * * * *

Did you hear about the Egyptian mummy that was pressed for time?

* * * * * * * * *

A Texan arriving at the gate of his eternal home remarked, "I never thought heaven would be so much like Texas." Replied Gabriel, "Son, this isn't heaven."

* * * * * * * * *

She was the self-appointed guardian of the village morals. Her chief complaint was the construction worker who parked his wheelbarrow at either the local tavern or in front of the local house of ill repute. Upon hearing the complaint, the man stifled all further complaints by leaving his wheelbarrow in front of the complaining lady's house overnight.

* * * * * * * * *

The husband came home with a big gash over his eyebrow, and his wife inquired, "What happened to you?"

"I bit myself," he replied.

"Impossible," she said.

"No, it wasn't, I had to stand on a chair to do it."

* * * * * * * * *

A lady was having real problems with her husband coming home drunk almost every night. She always met him at the door with a tongue lashing. In visiting with some of her neighbors, they told her that she was taking the wrong approach in dealing with her husband's problems. "When

121

he comes home next time," they told her, "have a sandwich ready for him and treat him very nicely."

She followed her friends' instructions. When her husband came home, she said, "I'm so happy to see you, dear, why don't we go in the kitchen and have a sandwich and visit a little bit."

He agreed.

Finally she said, "Let's go on upstairs to bed."

"Yes," he said, "we might just as well because when I get home I'm going to catch heck anyway."

* * * * * * * * *

MORTALITY

The applicant was asked what caused the death of his parents. He replied, "I don't recall, but I don't think it was anything serious."

* * * * * * * * *

A man applying for the position of insurance agent was asked what he thought was the normal mortality rate in the area to be served by the insurance company. He replied, "I really don't know, but I believe it averages about one per person."

* * * * * * * * *

Why is it that insurance people always talk about death benefits.

* * * * * * * * *

In the South, morticians are called Southern planters.

* * * * * * * * *

The other day I stole a kiss,
my conscience hurts alack,
I think I'll go tomorrow night
and put the darn thing back.

* * * * * * * * * *

The young man had a job with a company that required him to work the swing shift, from four in the afternoon until midnight. In going home after work, it was always necessary for him to walk around a cemetery that separated his home and his place of employment. One night when he was very tired, he decided to cut across the cemetery. On entering he discovered that there was a beaten path. It being very dark, he kept his feet right in the path, but he didn't know that a new grave had been dug in the center of the path, and of course he fell into it.

At first he was not too concerned, but when he realized that he could not get out because the hole was too deep, he became somewhat hysterical. Ultimately in complete exhaustion he sat down in the corner of the grave and fell asleep. Shortly thereafter the same fate befell another employee. He too went through the same antics of trying to get out. When he was just about to the exhaustion point the first employee woke up and shouted, "YOU CAN'T GET OUT OF HERE."

But he did.

* * * * * * * * * *

"Why," asked a young man of his professor, "should one become famous?" Beethoven, for example, was a great composer and what is he doing now? Decomposing.

* * * * * * * * * *

I bought my wife a piano but then traded it in for a clarinet. "Why?" he was asked. "With the clarinet, she can't sing."

* * * * * * * * * *

If you want to lead the band, you must face the music.

* * * * * * * * * *

Then there was the guy who listened to Lawrence Welk so long that he got drunk on bubbles.

* * * * * * * * * *

If you want to lead the band, you must face the music.

* * * * * * * * * *

Popular music does not stay popular very long. The other day a waiter dropped a tray of dishes and two couples got up to dance.

* * * * * * * * * *

A jitterbug is a fellow that has a wife, a note at the bank and a girl in the country all thirty days past due.

* * * * * * * * * *

Did you hear about the billy goat that ended it all. Seems he heard Frank Sinatra sing "There'll Never Be Another You".

* * * * * * * * * *

Next we will present a medley of three songs. One right after the other.

* * * * * * * * * *

The very best thing about rock and roll records is that if you break one side, the other breaks also.

* * * * * * * * * *

What do you call a musician that has just broken up with his girlfriend? Homeless.

* * * * * * * * * *

When country music is played backwards, you get back your wife (husband), your car, your mortgage on your house and return bus tickets from Branson, Missouri.

* * * * * * * * * *

He went out fit as a fiddle, but came home tight as a drum.

* * * * * * * * * *

Tonight we're going to sing three special numbers: "If you know Susie like I know Susie, you'll go out with Gertrude," and the second one will be, "I tried to look into her eyes, but they were too far apart."
And the last one will be, "Get out of the wheat field, Grandma, you're going against the grain."

* * * * * * * * * *

I can yodel but not out loud.

* * * * * * * * * *

OPTIMIST — PESSIMIST

He was so depressed that even the bad evening news on television cheered him up.

* * * * * * * * * *

There are some people who are never happy unless they are miserable.

* * * * * * * * * *

A pessimist's outlook on life: In the long run we are all dead.

* * * * * * * * * *

A bore is someone who when you ask how they are feeling tells you everything in detail.

* * * * * * * * * *

An pessimist is someone who thinks today is better than tomorrow.

* * * * * * * * * *

An optimist looks at a glass half-filled with water and says it's half full. The pessimist looking at the same glass says it is half empty.

* * * * * * * * * *

A man who had been condemned to die was brought before the king for final review and disposition. The defendant pleaded that he wanted to live and the king said, "I'll make you a proposition. If you teach my horse how to fly within one year, I'll set you free."

"Agreed," said the defendant.

"You're a fool," said his cellmates.

"No, I'm not," he shot back.

"How do you figure?" they asked him.

126

"Well," he said, "let's look at the odds. They just might be on my side. In a year," he said, "the king may die, the horse may die, or I may die, and then there's always the outside possibility that I will teach that horse how to fly."

* * * * * * * * * *

The optimist invented the airplane and the pessimist the parachute.

* * * * * * * * * *

All people smile in the same language.

* * * * * * * * * *

A pessimist may be one who has financed an optimist.

* * * * * * * * * *

The man living in an agricultural community kept telling everyone how terrible things were. It wasn't going to rain, there weren't going to be any crops, and the winter was going to be an extremely cold one. He was always a grouch. When folks saw him walking up one side of the street, they would automatically take the other side. One day one of the local residents went to the hospital with a heart attack. The pessimist thought that he ought to go see him. When he got there he found his friend lying under an oxygen tent. "It's too bad that you had a heart attack," said the pessimist, "but that's the way life is." This went on for some period of time and he finally concluded, "And now you're probably going to die."

And the patient under the oxygen tent simply responded, "I sure will, unless you take your foot off the oxygen tube!"

* * * * * * * * * *

OVERDOING

A young Catholic girl came home and told her mother excitedly that she had found a young man that she would like to marry. He was handsome, young, intelligent and his parents had a lot of money. There was only one thing wrong, the young man was not Catholic. The mother then told her to work real hard on this young man and convert him to their religion.

After some period of time the young daughter came home in tears and told her mother that there was not going to be a wedding.

"Why not?" asked the mother. "Did you not work hard to try to convert the young man to our faith?"

"Yes, Mom, I did. But I must have overdone it. He has decided to become a priest."

* * * * * * * * *

PETS

What happens to kittens that eat a ball of yarn? They have mittens.

* * * * * * * * *

There was the cat that ate some cheese and then waited for the mouse with baited breath.

* * * * * * * * *

In a pet shop the customer said, "I would like something for fleas." The clerk said, "Buy a dog."

* * * * * * * * *

I called my dog, Legion, because he stops at every post.

****

My dog saw a sign: "Wet Paint". So he did.

****

Why do fire trucks carry a dog? To find the fire hydrants.

****

I don't bother my husband with alarm clocks, I just open the door in the morning and throw the cat in.
How does that help wake him up?
He sleeps with the dog.

****

A farmer trained his dog to watch his watermelon patch. He called him Melancholy.

****

I call my dog, Waitress, he never comes when I call him.

****

Their dog is a member of the family, but I wonder which one?

****

A dog with three legs hopped into a police station and asked, "Who shot my paw?"

****

A customer said to the waitress, "This food is fit for a king." "Here King, here King."

****

A pet veterinarian and a taxidermist went into business together. They placed this motto above their door: "Either way, you get your pet back."

****

What's got four legs and barks?
A dog?
You heard it before.

* * * * * * * * * *

Who goes to bed with his shoes on?
A horse.

* * * * * * * * * *

"My cat can say it's own name."
"What is it?"
"Meow."

* * * * * * * * * *

PHILOSOPHY

Diogenes, a Greek, went out on a dark night in Athens looking for an honest man. When he got home he was asked, "Did you find an honest man?"
"No," he replied, "but I still have my lantern."

* * * * * * * * * *

It takes no talent to criticize.

* * * * * * * * * *

If you are undecided when you come to a fork in the road, take it.

* * * * * * * * * *

If one can profit from one's mistakes, many of us will have bright futures.

* * * * * * * * * *

The superior man blames himself. The inferior man blames others.

* * * * * * * * * *

The road to success is always under construction. - Wayne Pritchard

* * * * * * * * *

Mark Twain said, "If you pick up a starving dog and make him prosperous, he will not bite you. This is the principle difference between a dog and man."

* * * * * * * * *

You are either green and growing or ripe and rotting.
—Dr. Allen Unruh

* * * * * * * * *

Stretch the truth and it will snap back at you.

* * * * * * * * *

If there's anything I hate it's something that I don't like.

* * * * * * * * *

I suggest you clean your specs, you'll have a better outlook on life.

* * * * * * * * *

Patience is described as the ability to idle one's motor without stripping the gears.

* * * * * * * * *

Ozzie said, "One should always leave worrying up to a horse. They have bigger heads."

* * * * * * * * *

As you slide down the banister of life may all the splinters be pointed in the right direction.

* * * * * * * * *

If you lose the power to laugh, you lose the power to think. Humor loves company, joy requires it. Louie Warren

* * * * * * * * * *

Will Rogers said, "Live your life so that you wouldn't mind selling your pet parrot to your minister."

* * * * * * * * * *

You must share what you would keep,
Blessings from above.
They who cease to give will cease to keep,
That's the law of love.

—Author Unknown

* * * * * * * * * *

Troubles that are shared are halved; joys that are shared are doubled.

* * * * * * * * * *

Often your reasons are wrong, but your thinking is right. So do it.

* * * * * * * * * *

There is a German proverb that says, "It takes a great many shovelfuls to bury the truth."

* * * * * * * * * *

Always tell the truth because then you don't have to remember what you said.

* * * * * * * * * *

Dreams cannot come true if you oversleep.

* * * * * * * * * *

A young man asked Socrates if he should get married, and Socrates replied, "By all means, young man, get married. If you find a good wife you'll be happy. If you find a poor one, you'll be a philosopher."

* * * * * * * * * *

Socrates said that if every man and every woman would have to bring all of their problems and put them into a common heap from which each would have to take an equal portion, each would be willing to take his own and depart.

* * * * * * * * * *

If you come to the end of a perfect day, check again.

* * * * * * * * * *

If you dance with a grizzly bear, let him lead.

* * * * * * * * * *

The greatest thing in life is to trust and be trusted.

* * * * * * * * * *

It is better to give away your money while you're alive. It doesn't take any great generosity to give it away when you're dead.

* * * * * * * * * *

Everyone in the world is tolerant if you ask him.

* * * * * * * * * *

If we can't be thankful for what we receive, we should be thankful for what we escape.

* * * * * * * * * *

It is never safe to look into the future with eyes of fear.

* * * * * * * * * *

That was a tough question. It was almost like putting on a wet bathing suit.

* * * * * * * * *

Did you hear about the Senator who held hearings on the value of hearings?

* * * * * * * * *

Indecision is a form of hell on earth, but on the other hand, it might just be the key for flexibility, especially for politicians.

* * * * * * * * *

For some politicians, facts are irrelevant.

* * * * * * * * *

I've been told that if you want a friend when you go to Washington D. C. you should take a dog.

* * * * * * * * *

A bipartisan issue is a child born to a Republican father and a Democratic wife.

* * * * * * * * *

The problem with John Glenn's candidacy for president of the United States is that he had peaked too soon.

* * * * * * * * *

The reason politicians make strange bedfellows is because they usually share the same bunk.

* * * * * * * * *

This is my position. If you don't like it, I will change it.

* * * * * * * * *

Being lieutenant governor is like receiving maternity benefits when you are on social security.

* * * * * * * * *

The only fear that I have about growing older is that I'll lose my memory and be mistaken for a Senator.

* * * * * * * * *

A young man was asked what a politician was. He said, "It's someone who votes wrong, someone who polishes shoes, one who has a fever and goes out and tries to give the fever to everyone else."

* * * * * * * * *

A politician has a good chance of going to heaven - they say that hot air rises.

* * * * * * * * *

The bad thing about political jokes is that some might be elected.

* * * * * * * * *

People like politicians who say what they think so long as they think what they like.

* * * * * * * * *

Yes, I'm a politician. I stand on my record. If I didn't, someone would probably try to examine it.

* * * * * * * * *

Thank you very much for putting in your two cents worth. Here, you've got some change coming.

* * * * * * * * *

About Fanny Fox in the days of Wilbur Mills (Chairman of Ways & Means):
"She was only a stripper

At the Silver Slipper
But she had her ways and means."

* * * * * * * * * *

Churchill met a highly inebriated lady who said to him,
"If you were my husband, I would put poison into your tea."
Replied Churchill, "If you were my wife, I'd drink it.

* * * * * * * * * *

Any smart politician knows the best position is to the
right of the Democrats - left of the Republicans and directly
in front of the camera.

—Obren

* * * * * * * * * *

Some of my friends are for him and some of my friends
are against him, but I'm for my friends.

* * * * * * * * * *

A Republican at a political rally stated that his method of
getting extra votes was to give every taxi driver a large tip
and then tell them to vote Republican. "I think my way is
better," said a party colleague, "I give them no tip and tell
them to vote Democratic."

* * * * * * * * * *

Some politicians have trouble deciding whether they
were born in a log cabin or in a manger.

* * * * * * * * * *

The politician said, "I'm going to speak my mind
because I have nothing to lose."

* * * * * * * * * *

Did you hear the rumor about the smart politician?
There's no truth in it.

* * * * * * * * * *

Sir, I know where you are coming from, I only hope you have a return ticket.

* * * * * * * * *

We pay our senators $125,000 per year, plus amenities, and every six years they come around and ask for donations so that they can keep their jobs.

* * * * * * * * *

A politician is someone who approaches every subject with an open mouth.

* * * * * * * * *

There was a senator who wanted a bill calling for drug testing of all his fellow senators. One senator responded that he wouldn't mind that so long as the bill also would require an intelligence test as well.

* * * * * * * * *

A wise political philosopher once said, "If you can't understand it, oppose it."

* * * * * * * * *

The invitation to a political fund-raising dinner said, "$100 per plate (roquefort dressing 25 cents extra)."

* * * * * * * * *

Many politicians have presence of mind, but absence of thought."

* * * * * * * * *

There are three types of politicians: those that cannot lie, those that cannot tell the truth, and those that cannot tell the difference.

* * * * * * * * *

"What do you think of our two candidates?"
"Well, I'm glad only one can be elected."

A constituent told the candidate, "I wouldn't vote for you if you were St. Peter."

"If I were St. Peter," replied the candidate, "you couldn't vote for me—you wouldn't be in the same precinct."

****

Three rather worldly gentlemen were discussing what it meant to be important. The first one said that you would be important if you were invited to the White House for a talk with the president.

"No," said the second one, "you'd be really important if, while visiting the president, he received a call on the hot line and the president would not answer it."

"Still wrong," said the third. "You'd really be important if you're talking with the president when the hot line rings, and he answers it and says, 'It's for you'."

****

An appreciative candidate in the upper midwest put an ad into the local newspaper which read, "I want to thank the 400 citizens who encouraged me to run for office. I want to extend a special thanks to the 800 friends that promised to vote for me. I also want to thank the 200 that assured me that they did vote for me, and finally, a real vote of thanks to the 75 people who actually cast ballots for me in the recent election."

****

Two men flying on an airplane were discussing their imminent homecoming. Said the first, "I'm just out of prison and I know it's going to be tough." Said the second, "I know what you mean, I'm just getting home from Congress."

****

"You are my second choice."
"Who is your first?"
"Whoever announces his candidacy next."

* * * * * * * * * *

My friend is running for Mayor. He's never been a grafter. All he wants is a chance.

* * * * * * * * * *

I don't belong to any organized political party, I am a Republican (Democrat).

* * * * * * * * * *

I will run a clean campaign unless I can find something really juicy on my opponent.

* * * * * * * * * *

"Do you partake of intoxicating beverages?" inquired the constituent.
"Is that an inquiry or an invitation?" responded the candidate.

* * * * * * * * * *

You can tell a Republican (Democrat), but you can't tell him much.

* * * * * * * * * *

If re-elected I will promise to fulfill the promises that I made in the last campaign.

* * * * * * * * * *

"In the recent election, where did the turning point come?"
"Right after I threw my hat into the ring."

* * * * * * * * * *

HOW TO TELL REPUBLICANS FROM DEMOCRATS:
Republicans give their clothes to the less fortunate;

Democrats wear theirs. Republicans employ exterminators; Democrats step on bugs. Democrats buy most of the books that have been banned somewhere; Republicans form censorship committees and read them as a group. Republican boys date Democrat girls—they plan to marry Republican girls but they feel they're entitled to a little fun first. Republicans sleep in twin beds, some even in separate rooms; that's why there are more Democrats.

(From the Congressional Record, author unknown.)

* * * * * * * * * *

Both Theodore Roosevelt and John Kennedy have been credited with the following: The credit belongs to the man actually in the arena whose face is marred by dust and sweat and blood . . . who knows the great enthusiasm . . . the great devotion to duty . . . and spends himself in a worthy cause.

Who at best if he wins knows the thrill of high achievement, and if he fails, at least he fails while daring greatly . . . His place shall never be with those cold and timid souls who know neither victory nor defeat.

* * * * * * * * * *

"You'll get the vote of every thinking person."
"Fine—but I need a majority."

* * * * * * * * * *

Quitters never win and winners never quit.

* * * * * * * * * *

A politician is a man full of promise.

* * * * * * * * * *

In this campaign I want you to know that my wife is not a side issue.

* * * * * * * * * *

Before Columbus discovered America there were no taxes, no Democrats, no Republicans, no energy crises, no TV commercials, plenty of fish, no pollution, and women did all the work. And now we have politicians who want to improve on that?

****

What are the three major parties?
Democrat, Republican and cocktail.

****

I'm a confused independent.

****

Political ignorance: When you don't know something and someone finds it out.

****

Primary: The political dating game.

****

Russian Medical Bulletin!
President Boris Yeltsin's condition has been upgraded from plateaued to plastered.

****

After 1994 Election
This is first time since my wedding day that the republications have been on top.

****

POLLS

A psychologist took a poll surveying just how people sat in their tubs. He discovered that out of a hundred people, 99 sat facing the faucets. Only one sat facing away from the faucets. They asked the lone man why and he said, "Very simple, I have no plug for my tub."

****

POPULATION CONTROL

The reason California has earthquakes is because so many of its citizens forget to take their earth control pills.

****

Then there was the secretary who dropped her birth control pill in the xerox machine and it would not reproduce.

****

As the last member of a family of 12, I have mixed emotions about this business of population control.

****

The government is concerned about the population explosion, and the population is concerned about government explosion.

****

If your parents didn't have children, chances are you won't either.

****

Emcees are not made—that's why some people advo-
cate birth control.

****

Population control
would be more effective,
If it could be made
retroactive.

****

"Do you know what the best form of birth control in the
world is?"
"No."
"That's it."

****

POVERTY

During the Great Depression we were so poor that we
were able to put our socks on from either end.

****

I came from a family of plenty - plenty of poverty.

****

Unless you are poor you will never know the luxury of
getting.

****

A beggar asked a man for $10. The man reached in his
wallet and took out a five dollar bill and gave it to the beggar. Where upon the beggar replied, "Didn't I ask you for
$10?"

"That's right," replied the man, "this way we break even. You lose $5 and I lose $5."

* * * * * * * * *

We were so poor that we could afford rickets in only one leg.

* * * * * * * * *

Times were so tough that when we hitchhiked, we'd take a ride either way.

* * * * * * * * *

The poor seek food, the rich seek appetites.

* * * * * * * * *

Times were so tough that when Dad said grace, he kept both hands over the butter plate.

* * * * * * * * *

My dad couldn't wait for the depression of 1929. He started ours in 1928.

* * * * * * * * *

During the depression, the fellow ordered a bowl of soup in the restaurant, and as he was about to eat it, a fly fell in the soup. So he carefully fished it out, and holding the fly's right wing between his right thumb and forefinger, and the fly's left wing between his left thumb and forefinger, he said, "Now, darnit, spit it out."

* * * * * * * * *

A speaker told his audience that the United States is bordered on the north by Canada by the Atlantic on the east and by the Pacific on the west. Then he inquired, "How old am I?" A member of the audience got up, "You're 44 years old." He said, "How were you able to guess?"

"Well my brother is half crazy and he is only 22."

* * * * * * * * *

An American tourist in Mexico City took a taxi. The taxi driver went through a red light where upon the American tapped the driver on the shoulder and said, "Hey, you just went through a red light." "Not to worry," replied the taxi driver, "I do it all the time and nothing ever happens." They went along a little further and he went through another red light. Again the American tapped him on the shoulder and said, "Hey, you just went through another red light."

"Not to worry, I do it all the time nothing ever happens." Then he came up to a green light and the taxi driver stopped, so the American inquired, "Why in the world do you go through two red lights and then stop at a green one?"

"Well," replied the taxi driver, "I think my brother, he is coming."

* * * * * * * * *

A relative is the kin you love to touch.

* * * * * * * * *

I have so many relatives that they're coming out of the woodwork.

* * * * * * * * *

"I took the deduction," said the taxpayer to the Internal Revenue agent, "because my relatives are an organized charity."

145

****

A large family was finally able to move into a more spacious home. Sometime later an uncle asked his nephew, "How do you like your new house?"

"Just fine," replied the lad. "My brother and I have our own rooms, and so do my sisters. But poor Mom, she's still stuck in the same room with Dad."

****

I trace my ancestry all the way back to the Boston Tea Party. It was my great-great Aunt Ella. She was the last bag that they threw into the ocean.

****

RELIGION

The rabbi loved to play golf but was reluctant to play in his home town on the Sabbath Day so he'd drive to a course out in the country.

St. Gabriel and St. Peter felt this was unbecoming to a rabbi or a man of the cloth, so they decided to punish him.

The rabbi teed off and sliced the ball and the ball hit a tree. Then Gabriel wiggled his finger and the ball turned, landed on the green and dropped in for a hole in one.

"What kind of punishment is that?" asked St. Peter. St. Gabriel replied, "Who is the rabbi going to tell?"

****

A professor at a seminary asked a student to name three members of the cloth.

The student replied, "Hart, Shaffner, and Marx."

****

The title of my speech is, "The World and Other Things".

In the beginning God created heaven and earth, day and night, man and animals and that leads me to my subject.

* * * * * * * * *

Here's the story of how Pope Paul from Poland was selected by the Cardinals. They had been deadlocked and could not reach a decision until one of the Cardinals asked his fellow Cardinals to take a Pole.

* * * * * * * * *

A newly ordained minister was about to deliver his first major sermon to his congregation. He was somewhat apprehensive and as he stepped into the pulpit, he announced, "Behold I come." Then his throat went dry and he stepped back and tried it again. Again he said, "Behold I come." Then stepping back he tried a third time and in his exuberance he overshot the pulpit. A baby being held by his mother began to cry and the Reverend began an apology. The lady responded, "You need not apologize, after all, I had three warnings."

* * * * * * * * *

In our church we do not have ten commandments. We have only five and five suggestions.

* * * * * * * * *

If all the people in our church could be laid end to end they would all be more comfortable.

* * * * * * * * *

Some people coming away from hearing a good sermon are inspired, others awaken much refreshed.

* * * * * * * * *

Reading the Congressional Record can be a very religious experience - it passeth all understanding.

****

A church needed someone to ring the bell in the belfry on Sunday mornings. After advertising for the position, no one showed up except one young person without arms. The church administrator questioned his ability to ring the bell, but the young fellow proved that he could do it just by using his head. So one Sunday morning he over did it and he fell from the belfry and landed on the steps in front of the church. In viewing the body, a bypasser inquired who the person was. A member of the congregation responded, "I don't really know, but his face rings a bell."

****

A contractor painting the steeple on a church ran out of paint as he neared the top so he thinned it so he could finish the painting job. It was not long before the thin portion began to peel. He was called before the church administrators and confessed that he thinned the paint as he neared the top. So the senior pastor of the church admonished him to go out, repaint and thin no more.

****

A young man entering the monastery was told that he could speak only two words at the end of each ten-year period. At the end of the first ten-year period the head monk asked the young monk what he had to say. He replied, "Bad food." Ten years later he was asked again what he had to say. He answered, "Hard bed." At the end of the third period he was asked again if he had anything to say and he said, "I quit!" So the head monk simply said, "You might just as well because all you've done since coming here is complain for the past thirty years."

****

A parishioner informed his pastor that he had just won two million dollars in the lottery. The minister replied, "That's sinful, you had better not accept it."

"But Reverend," said the lucky lottery winner, "I'm giving half of it to the church." The reverend keeled over, dead.

* * * * * * * * * *

Many were called but few could make it.

* * * * * * * * * *

"Doctor," inquired a patient, "is there anything you can do to cure me of my snoring?"
"Does it disturb your wife?" asked the Doc. "No, Doc, it only embarrasses her. It is the rest of the congregation that is disturbed."

* * * * * * * * * *

Upon reading the Bible, the reader came upon this verse: "Judas went out and hung himself." He wanted to read something more uplifting so he turned some pages and read: "Go and do likewise."

* * * * * * * * * *

Don't be so heavenly that you are no earthly good.

* * * * * * * * * *

Sign in the church: No Smoking in the Sanctuary - Sancu very much.

* * * * * * * * * *

When Congress is in session the Chaplin does not pray for the Congressmen, rather he prays for the Country.

* * * * * * * * * *

The husband upon returning from church was asked by his wife if the minister had delivered a good sermon. "Yes," he replied. "What was it about," she asked. He said, "He preached on sin."
"What did he say about it?"
"He was against it."

* * * * * * * * * *

A minister: Thank God it's Monday.

* * * * * * * * *

A minister went bear hunting with his friend in Montana. Finally they spotted a big grizzly bear. The minister got so excited he dropped his gun and started to run with the grizzly in hot pursuit. Finally, being exhausted the minister stopped and looked at the bear. He said, "Dear Lord, I pray that this is a Christian bear." The bear got down on his forepaws and prayed, "Dear Lord, bless this food which I am about to eat."

* * * * * * * * *

A good Sunday sermon is one where the minister does not refer directly to me.

* * * * * * * * *

Appearing at the Pearly Gates, Saint Peter said to the newly arrived gentleman that he could not enter until he gave the name of the Son of God. The gentleman replied, "Andy."

"Andy? How did you ever arrive at that name?"

"Well," he said, "And he walks with me, and he talks with me and he tells me I am His own."

* * * * * * * * *

God was asked if there would ever be an American pope. God replied, "Probably."

"What about an Italian pope?"

"That's a possibility."

"What about another Polish pope?" Replied God, "Not in my lifetime."

* * * * * * * * *

The young Mexican was apprehended as he crossed the Rio Grande into the United States. The officer went through the Mexican's knapsack and found a bottle of liquid. The Mexican said it was Holy Water. He had just come from the shrine across the river. Then the officer took some of the liquid and smelled of it. He said, "Young man, this smells and tastes like tequila."

"Another miracle," replied the Mexican.

****

I was born a Lutheran, raised a Lutheran and I'm always going to be a Lutheran. Nobody's going to make a Christian out of me.

****

I never work on Sundays
Except for the Lord, said the man.
The pay is rather nominal
But I sure like the retirement plan.

****

At the annual meeting of the congregation a member got up and said, "I again make a motion against the church buying a chandelier. First, nobody knows how to spell it and wouldn't know to order it. Secondly, when they did get it, nobody would know how to play it. Thirdly, what the church really needs is more lights so everybody can see and sing the hymns."

****

A bystander was asked, "Are you a Jehovah Witness?" "No," he replied. "I didn't even see the accident."

****

A highly inebriated passenger sat next to a priest on an airline trip and immediately asked the priest, "Sir, could you tell me what causes arthritis?" The priest responded, "It's caused by drinking, running around with wild women and generally not taking care of your health." The inebriated person seemed to be listening and then sat quietly for a pretty good period. Then the priest turned to the inebriated fellow and said, "Oh, why did you really want to know what causes arthritis?"

"Well," he said, "I read in the paper this morning where the Pope has arthritis in both knees."

* * * * * * * * *

Roy asked Isadore why he hit him. "Because," he replied "you crucified our leader." Isadore said, "But that was nearly 2000 years ago."

"Yes," said Roy, "but I just heard about it yesterday."

* * * * * * * * *

Pat said to Mike, "Liquor, gambling and fast women have always been my enemies. But when the Pope came to Ireland, he said we should all love our enemies."

* * * * * * * * *

A Catholic returning from Mass one Sunday morning found his buddies still sleeping. It was a very cold morning. He said to himself, "Wouldn't it be hell if I were wrong."

* * * * * * * * *

Blessed are they who travel in circles for they shall be called wheels.

* * * * * * * * *

"Reverend," said the Texan, "that was a damn good sermon."

Where upon the Reverend replied, "You shouldn't swear."

The Texan said, "Well I thought it was so good I put $1,000 in the plate."

Where upon the Reverend responded, "The hell you did."

* * * * * * * * *

The reverend told his congregation that he heard there was one man who had been carrying on with another man's wife. To repent he suggested that the person put $10 in the collection plate. When the collection plate was brought forward there were nine $10 bills and one $5 with a note attached, I will bring the balance next week.

* * * * * * * * * *

The minister had his car towed to a local garage for repairs. The minister told the mechanic, "I hope that you won't charge me too much. After all I'm just a poor preacher."

"I know," came back the mechanic, "I've heard you."

* * * * * * * * * *

The young Catholic boy and the young Jewish boy were arguing as to whether priests or rabbis were the smartest. The young Jewish boy finally conceded to the Catholic boy by stating, "The priest should be because you tell him everything."

* * * * * * * * * *

The Irish priest told Pat that everyone in his congregation would ultimately die. Pat began to laugh. "Why are you laughing?" asked the priest. Replied Pat, "I'm not a member of this congregation."

* * * * * * * * * *

It was so dry that even Baptists had to resort to sprinkling.

* * * * * * * * * *

Item in a church bulletin: Our minister is leaving the church this Sunday. Will you please send in a small donation. The congregation wants to give him a little momentum.

* * * * * * * * * *

A young man worked for a lumber company. He was a very good man, but he had one bad habit. Each night when

153

he finished work he would put a piece of lumber into his truck. Soon he had a big pile of lumber. Finally his conscience began to bother him. And being Catholic he went to see his priest and confessed everything. Father listened very intently and then said, "Young man, you have done something very, very serious. You're going to have to make a novena. Do you know what a novena is?"

"No, Father," he said, "I sure don't, but if you've got the plans, I've got the lumber."

* * * * * * * * * *

The pastor said there were 250 sins, so one of the parishioners wrote in for the list.

* * * * * * * * * *

The Sunday School lesson was on honesty. The teacher inquired of his class, "Would all those of you who read the 35th chapter of Matthew raise your right hand?" A number of them raised their hands. And then he said, "You are the ones I want to talk to. There is no 35th chapter of Matthew."

* * * * * * * * * *

Little Jimmy was attending his first Sunday School class. "Do you say your prayers before eating?" inquired his teacher. "I don't have to," responded the boy, "my mother is a good cook."

* * * * * * * * * *

The visiting pastor put fifty cents in the collection plate as it was passed. As he departed from the church after the service, the head usher handed him the collection plate and stated that it was customary for his church to give the pastor the entire offering. When he looked in the plate, there he saw his own fifty cent piece. The moral of this story is, that had he put more into it, he would have gotten more out of it.

* * * * * * * * * *

The church was having trouble raising its annual budget. A member of the congregation, an electrician, came up with a great idea. He said, "We will wire all of the seats, and then when our chairman of fund raising asks for pledges on Sunday morning, we will follow something like the following procedure. Will all those who will pledge $5 per week please stand up? And then I will punch the $5 button."

They went through this procedure up to what they felt would be the maximum limits of some to pledge. After the congregation had been dismissed, in the back row they found that the only Scotch member of the congregation had been electrocuted.

* * * * * * * * *

"You must repent or die," said the minister. Whereupon a visitor to the church said, "I'm sure glad I'm not a member of this church."

* * * * * * * * *

Sign on a church bulletin board: If you don't like what you hear on a given Sunday, your sins will be cheerfully refunded.

* * * * * * * * *

A man who had been living a high life decided that he wanted to repent. So he went to the Baptist Church and asked to be baptized. The minister performed the rites of immersion in front of the congregation. When he came up out of the water the newly baptized man said that he felt so great that he was going to give ten percent of everything he earned to the church. Whereupon the reverend replied, "We have a tither in our tank."

* * * * * * * * *

Asked to draw a picture of the biblical flight into Egypt, a boy drew a plane with four people in it flying toward Egypt. Three of the passengers had halos.

"Who are they?" inquired the Sunday School teacher.

"They are Jesus, Mary and Joseph," replied the boy.
"And who is the one without the halo?"
"That is Pontius the Pilot," replied the boy.

* * * * * * * * * *

Three nuns were each given $100. The first nun said the she wanted to give hers to some Catholic youth organization; the next stipulated that hers might go to a child welfare organization; and the third nun said she was going out on the street and give it to the first person she ran into that really looked like he needed it.

She went down the street and the first guy she met was an elderly fellow who was dressed in very shabby clothes, so she thrust the $100 bill into the palm of his hand. She became choked up and really couldn't say anything except, "Godspeed."

Two days later this fellow appeared at the convent and said that he wanted to see the nun that had given him a $100 bill. He tried to describe her and said that he really didn't know how to describe a nun but, anyway, he surmised that it was Sister Helena.

When she got to the door, the man said he was so grateful for what she had done the other day that he went to the races and Godspeed had come in first. And he gave her $800.00

* * * * * * * * * *

A minister, in administering the confirmation rites for an elderly new member, asked, "Do you repent of the devil and all of his ways?" The member replied, "In my position, I can't afford to antagonize anyone."

* * * * * * * * * *

A lady buying a broiled chicken sandwich at the Dairy Queen was asked by the clerk whether she intended to eat it there or take with her. She replied, "I hope to do both."

****

Do you know why a Norwegian hits the salt shaker on the bottom and the Swede hits the shaker on the side?
Sure. To get the salt out.

****

"What's that fly doing in my soup."
"I think the back stroke, sir."

****

Everything on the menu looked high priced so the young man asked his date, "What will you have my dear plump little doll?"

****

The lamb was a little tough - Oh, let's not talk chop.

****

He was so frugal that when he and his wife went out to dinner he asked for separate checks.

****

The waitress was taking an order from two men that were having lunch. The one said, "I want a glass of weak tea." The second said, "I want tea also, but make mine strong and be sure that it is in a clean glass." When the waitress returned with the tea she inquired, "which one of you asked for the clean glass?"

****

"What would you like for dinner tonight, dear? Steak, roast beef, baked ham or would you rather stay home and have hash?"

* * * * * * * * *

My wife must be a good cook. When I came home the other night I found three truck drivers at our house eating dinner.

* * * * * * * * *

"Waiter, bring me some of your spumoni vermicelli that's on the menu."
"Sorry, sir, that's the proprietor."

* * * * * * * * *

Sign in a restaurant window: If you don't eat here, we'll both starve.

* * * * * * * * *

Don't criticize a man for flirting with the waitress — he may be playing for big steaks.

* * * * * * * * *

The public health service reports that there are at least 40 million overweight people in the United States. Those are round figures, of course.

* * * * * * * * *

In the coffee shop a traveling salesman summoned a waitress and gave her his order, "Two eggs and fry them very hard, two slices of toast burned black, and a cup of cold coffee.
"I can't do that for you," the waitress said.
"The heck you can't," replied the customer. "You did it for me yesterday."

* * * * * * * * *

The wife said to her husband at a buffet dinner, "That's the third time you've gone back for more chicken. Doesn't that embarrass you?"

"No, dear," he said, "I keep telling them I'm getting it for you."

****

"I don't like all these flies that are flying around here."

"Well, just point out the ones you do like, sir, and I'll swat the rest."

****

Waiter: I have stewed kidneys, fried liver, and pigs feet.

Customer: Don't tell me all your troubles—just bring me a bowl of soup and a turkey sandwich.

****

SALESMEN

After his company merged with a larger one, he came home and asked his wife, "If I lost my job and became penniless, would you still love me?"

"Yes, dear," she replied. "And I would also miss you."

****

He must have been a super-salesman. He sold a suit to the undertaker with two pair of pants.

****

The salesman was caught up in a big blizzard in Ohio so he wired his boss, "I'm stranded due to a very heavy snowstorm. Please wire instructions." Came back the reply from his boss, "start your vacation immediately."

159

* * * * * * * * *

Commenting on his profession the salesman said, "I've stayed in more hotel rooms than the Gideon Bible."

* * * * * * * * *

I didn't want to tell my boss that I was the greatest salesman that he ever had. I really didn't want to tell him that, but I felt that I should tell the truth since I was under oath.

* * * * * * * * *

A formula for success in making house to house calls is after knocking and the lady comes to the door, you inquire, "Miss, is your mother in?"

* * * * * * * * *

Always tell me why it can be done, never tell me why it cannot be done.

* * * * * * * * *

I've been leading a dog's life, traveling from pole to pole.

* * * * * * * * *

Living a double life will get you nowhere twice as fast.

* * * * * * * * *

Even if you're on the right track, you can be run over if you just sit there.

* * * * * * * * *

A town located a mile off the main highway west of the Paul Revere town of Boston was having great difficulties. The city fathers met time and time again to revive the community's economy. But all to no avail.

One day a young salesman showed up and told the city fathers, "I have the solution."

"What is it?" They inquired.

"We must put a billboard up out at the junction of the highway."

They replied, "We already have a billboard there."

"In that case," said the salesman, "we'll have to change the copy."

The salesman was authorized to change the copy and after he did business began to boom. On the billboard he put these words: THIS IS THE ROAD THAT PAUL REVERE WOULD HAVE TAKEN HAD HE COME THIS WAY.

* * * * * * * * * *

The hotel clerk told the salesman that there were no more rooms with bath, and would he mind sharing a bath with another man.

"No," said the salesman, "not as long as he stays at his end of the tub."

* * * * * * * * * *

The greatest salesman that I ever heard of was a milking machine salesman. He went out to see a farmer who had only one cow, sold him two milking machines and took the cow as a down payment.

* * * * * * * * * *

You cannot automate a salesman.

* * * * * * * * * *

The man who rolls up his sleeves seldom loses his shirt.

* * * * * * * * * *

Why complain about your troubles? They're the reason for half your income.

* * * * * * * * * *

Most everything is difficult the first time.

* * * * * * * * * *

The average guy is as close to the bottom as he is to the top.

* * * * * * * * * *

You can get business by asking for it.

* * * * * * * * * *

The greatest underdeveloped territory in the world is under your own hat.

* * * * * * * * * *

Eighty-five percent of all successful sales come after the fifth call.

* * * * * * * * * *

Nothing happens until a sale is made.

* * * * * * * * * *

We're going to have another sales contest. The first prize will be that you get to keep your job.

* * * * * * * * * *

It's not your aptitude, but rather your attitude that determines your altitude in life.

* * * * * * * * * *

SECRETARIES

The boss said to his secretary, "You should have been here at eight o'clock this morning."
"Why?" asked the secretary. "What happened?"

* * * * * * * * * *

This is the earliest you've ever been late.

* * * * * * * * * *

I don't have a private secretary because I don't have a private office.

* * * * * * * * * *

My secretary doesn't smoke, drink or gamble—her other bad habits don't leave her enough time.

* * * * * * * * * *

The successful secretary is the pretty young thing who can think like a man, look like a lady and work like a dog.

* * * * * * * * * *

Some Congressmen believe in life, liberty, and the pursuit of secretaries.

* * * * * * * * * *

SERVICE AND SERVICE CLUBS

The Bill of Rights gives us many rights. Maybe the most important one was not spelled out, namely, the freedom to care.

* * * * * * * * * *

What you do for yourself dies with you. What you do for others may live into immortality.

* * * * * * * * * *

He who takes
But never gives
May last for years
But never lives.

* * * * * * * * * *

163

The young boy remarked to his friend, "My Dad is an Elk, an Eagle, a Moose and a Lion. Asked the boy, "How much does it cost to see him?"

* * * * * * * * * *

The president of a local Lions Club stated that there were 240,000 people in the United States over ninety and 13,000 over 100. After making this observation he stated, "I thought there were more Rotarians than that."

* * * * * * * * * *

The best way to forget your own problems is to help someone else.

* * * * * * * * * *

Service to others is the rent we pay for the privilege of living on this planet.

* * * * * * * * * *

Let us be kind to one another — we are all fighting a tough battle.

* * * * * * * * * *

The fun in life comes in the doing.

* * * * * * * * * *

The best exercise is to bend down and help someone up.

* * * * * * * * * *

"If every man's internal cares
Were printed on his brow
How many would his pity share
That have his envy now."

* * * * * * * * * *

A young lady lit up a cigarette after finishing her lunch. An elderly lady sitting near by turned to the young lady and huffingly said, "I'd rather commit adultery than to be seen smoking in public." Replied the young lady, "I would too, but I have only thirty minutes."

* * * * * * * * * *

The fellow who was in an anti-smoking campaign looked at one of the visitors and said, "Look at those fingers, they are all yellow." "Yes, I know. I'm Chinese."

* * * * * * * * * *

If it weren't for my cough caused by my excessive smoking, I wouldn't get any exercise at all.

* * * * * * * * * *

Smoking won't take you to hell, you'll just smell like you've been there.

* * * * * * * * * *

I've read so much about the bad effects of smoking that I've decided to quit reading.

* * * * * * * * * *

A fellow showed up for work with his hand all bandaged up.

"Whatever happened?"

"Last night I was downtown getting some cigars and a clumsy old fool stepped on my hand."

* * * * * * * * * *

SPEAKER

I want to irritate my question.

* * * * * * * * * *

He wasn't the best speaker we ever had but he sure stayed with us the longest.

* * * * * * * * * *

In addressing you today, I'm going to use the Vitamin B approach. I'll be brief. I'll be seated. Then I'll be gone.

* * * * * * * * * *

There's nothing wrong with having nothing to say unless you insist on saying it.

* * * * * * * * * *

After receiving a rather lengthy introduction, the speaker said, "Now aren't you glad that I have not accomplished more?"

* * * * * * * * * *

When I made my first public speech I was so nervous that I could have thread a sewing machine while it was running and my throat was so dry that I couldn't even squeak.

* * * * * * * * * *

I only worry about the first five minutes of my speech. Research has shown that after the first five minutes most members of an audience tune out the speaker and engage in sexual fantasies.

* * * * * * * * * *

My last speech was really a good one. Halfway through my speech I saw lots of people get up to go home to get their friends.

* * * * * * * * * *

The speaker was unequivocally ambivalent.

* * * * * * * * *

As he was raising the microphone, the speaker said, "Excuse me while I adjust this microphone for inflation."

* * * * * * * * *

"Did he put enough fire into his speech?"
"No, he could have put more of his speech into the fire."

* * * * * * * * *

Upon receiving a flowery introduction the speaker said, "You may now raise your eyes and look upon me."

* * * * * * * * *

I'm normally quite abrupt
But when I'm praised I don't interrupt.

* * * * * * * * *

Charm, wit and levity
May help one at the start
But in the end it's brevity
That wins the public's heart.

* * * * * * * * *

After making a somewhat lengthy speech, the speaker looked at his watch. Then a member of the audience in the front row said to the speaker, "Did your watch stop, also?"

* * * * * * * * *

After being introduced into a seated audience, "Thanks for the applause. You can all sit down now."

* * * * * * * * *

I hope our speaker can dazzle us with his brevity.

* * * * * * * * *

"Must you always go to sleep when I begin to speak."
"No, it's entirely voluntary."

* * * * * * * * *

Our speaker tonight has the respect of intelligent men, he's got mine.

* * * * * * * * *

"My score for a speaker
Goes up a few notches
When he speaks with a watch
That he frequently watches.

But it's lowered again
When before he gets through
He's got us all watching
Our own watches, too."

—Robert Orben

* * * * * * * * *

We like a finished speaker,
We really, really do.
Not one who is polished,
But one who's finally through."

* * * * * * * * *

This is going to be a very brief introduction because there aren't too many good things that you can say about our speaker.

* * * * * * * * *

I'm not going to bore you with a long speech. I can do it with a short one.

* * * * * * * * *

A joke loses its punch when the punch line becomes apparent.

* * * * * * * * *

Well go ahead and speak your mind, you have nothing to lose.

****

An invited speaker was pacing up and down in the restroom and a lady said, "Are you nervous?"

"Nope, never," said the guest.

"Then what are you doing in the ladies restroom?" she inquired.

****

The only person that I can think of that has never been plagiarized must have been Adam.

****

Looking over his audience the speaker said, "If each four of you had brought a fifth this would have been a much better crowd."

****

When talking, be as brief as when you are making a will. The fewer the words, the less chances for litigation.

****

Sometimes we forget to turn off the sound when our minds go blank.

****

Do not engage mouth until brain is in gear.

****

"Do you believe in free speech?"

"I most certainly do."

"Then why don't you come to our town next week and give us a free talk at the Rotary Club?"

****

I've had a request—but I will speak anyway.

****

You've been a wonderful audience, you stayed.

****

Apple pie and speeches are improved with shortening.

****

There is an old proverb that says, "If I listen, I have the advantage. If I speak, others have it."

****

If you are a poor speaker, don't tell everyone. They will find out soon enough.

****

If you ask me how long it will take to prepare a 15-minute speech, my answer will be six hours. If you ask me how long it would take me to prepare a two-hour speech, I'd tell you that I am ready now.

****

Some speakers are good. Some speakers are lousy. I'm good and lousy.

****

Mine is a low-budget talk.

****

I guess I'm going to return for another speech. I just got a note saying it would be a cold night before they would have me back again.

****

Gladstone said that a speech need not be eternal to be immortal.

****

It's un-American not to speak when invited to do so.

* * * * * * * * * *

Our speaker needs no introduction, he just needs a conclusion.

* * * * * * * * * *

Our emcee must be a gentleman. The room from which he emerged proclaimed him so.

* * * * * * * * * *

I could have listened to that introduction all evening, and for awhile I thought I would have to.

* * * * * * * * * *

Who needs talent with courage like that?

* * * * * * * * * *

I have traded many a poor speech for a good meal.

* * * * * * * * * *

A gingerale speaker is one that goes flat after being uncorked for a few minutes.

* * * * * * * * * *

Thank you for the applause. It was scattered but sincere.

* * * * * * * * * *

Blessed are they who expect nothing for they shall not be disappointed.

* * * * * * * * * *

This looks like a father-daughter banquet.

* * * * * * * * * *

I was asked if I gave the same speech wherever I go.
I said, "Yes."
"Doesn't this present a problem when you are invited back?" asked one of my friends.
"No," I replied, "I've never been asked back."

* * * * * * * * *

The obstetrician told the expectant mother, "I hope that you have a better delivery than your husband."

* * * * * * * * *

SPORTS

Why did Billy Martin request cremation when he died? He wanted to be fired just one more time.

* * * * * * * * *

Who gets more hits in New York than the Yankees? The Mafia.

* * * * * * * * *

If a husband is plucked in his rocking chair before the TV set and watches four football games in succession, the wife has a right to declare him legally dead.

* * * * * * * * *

Old quarterbacks never die, they just fade back and pass away.

* * * * * * * * *

A football fanatic is one who tries to make both weekends meet.

* * * * * * * * *

A teacher asked her students to list the names of eleven important Americans. After a waiting period, the teacher asked Jimmy, "Would you read your list to the class?" Jimmy said, "I can't just yet because I can't think of the fullback's name."

The end of the fifth round was going badly for the challenger in the heavyweight boxing contest, so the manager whispered into the staggering boxer's ear, "The next time he hits you, hit him back."

* * * * * * * * *

Sinus was the reason my brother, Ozzie and I never played professional football. Nobody would sign us up.

* * * * * * * * *

When Babe Ruth was asked why he earned more money than the President, Mr. Ruth replied, "Well, I think I had a better year than Hoover."

* * * * * * * * *

I could have been center on the football team except for the fact that I am ticklish.

* * * * * * * * *

Speaking about our football team, we lost once in awhile - in fact almost once a week.

* * * * * * * * *

The alumni told us they would be with us, win or tie.

* * * * * * * * *

"After a bad season, I was speaking to the Touchdown Club. The president of the college told me it was not good-bye, it was not so long, not auf Wiedersehen, but as I disappeared, I noted a piece of mistletoe had been attached to the seat of my trousers."

—Coach Bob Devany

* * * * * * * * *

"Coaching is a precarious business — one coach had two bad years and then was pronounced dead."

—Coach Bob Devany

* * * * * * * * *

Two umpires were talking about how they umpired a game. The first said they may be strikes or balls, but he always called them as he saw them. The second said, "As far as I'm concerned, they are neither strikes or balls until I say what they are."

* * * * * * * * *

A seven year old told his mother that he was the world's greatest batter. "Just watch me." He throws up ball after ball and misses and misses again and again. Then he turns to his mother and states, "At least I'm the world's greatest pitcher."

* * * * * * * * *

During my youth I wore boxer shorts — but only for a brief time.

* * * * * * * * *

Why can't a Cheetah beat a Gazelle in a race? Because no one ever wins when they cheetah.

* * * * * * * * *

Some teenagers were talking about baseball. One asked the other, "By the way, who was this lady Babe Ruth anyway?"

* * * * * * * * *

A Little League baseball game was underway when a late-arriving spectator inquired as to the score.
"Twenty to nothing," replied a Little Leaguer.
"They're beating you bad," said the spectator.
"No, not really, we haven't been up to bat yet."

* * * * * * * * *

A football team is eleven men and a bookie.

* * * * * * * * *

A winner must first know what losing's like. - M.S. Forbes

* * * * * * * * * *

I always umpired because I couldn't see well enough to bat.

* * * * * * * * * *

Babe Ruth said, "Stopping at third base adds no more to the score than striking out."

* * * * * * * * * *

A young lad said that baseball reminds him of his family, with mother pitching, dad catching, everyone taking a turn at bat, and the kids doing most of the fielding.

* * * * * * * * * *

In the David and Goliath story, we learn that Goliath probably had pituitary gland troubles. He stood nine feet, nine inches tall. He was a good-sized athlete and could have played on any team. But when David met him, he Nolan Ryan'd a fast one and hit the giant right between the eyes. And the giant probably said, "I've never had anything like that enter my head before."

* * * * * * * * * *

A coach, because of the very poor win-loss record, was forced out of his position. Before relinquishing his office, he decided to leave two envelopes to his successor, and attached a note, "If things start going tough, you open the first envelope."

The successor was having a very bad season. He decided to open the first envelope, and it simply read, "Blame your predecessor."

As the season progressed, there was no improvement, so he decided to open the second envelope. In it was this note: "Make out two envelopes."

* * * * * * * * * *

The trouble with being a good sport is that you have to lose to prove it.

* * * * * * * * * *

STOCK MARKET

My broker and I have drifted apart
From now on I will take my advice from a dart.

* * * * * * * * * *

With the stock market on the decline, bars are serving a new drink called Stocks on the Rocks.

* * * * * * * * * *

Will Rogers was asked if he had any advice concerning the stock market. "Yes," he said. "buy stock that goes up, then sell it. If it doesn't go up, don't buy it."

* * * * * * * * * *

Noah was a successful financier. He floated his stock and liquidated everyone else's.

* * * * * * * * * *

When a friend asked Bernard Baruch whether the stock market would go up or down, he simply replied, "Undoubtedly."

* * * * * * * * * *

The bulls get a little, the bears get a little, but the hogs get nothing.

* * * * * * * * * *

Did you hear about the investor who is taking a course in veterinary medicine so that he will be able to look after the cats and dogs he bought in the recent bull market?

* * * * * * * * * *

The market gyrates and I don't care
For I'm neither bull nor bear.
I make no foolish fiscal bets,
All my money's tied up in debts.

* * * * * * * * * *

"What do you think of getting measles at 71?"
"You think you got problems? I got Penn Central at 72."

* * * * * * * * *

You never lose when you make a profit.

* * * * * * * * * *

A Canadian called his American friend and said that he had a hundred shares in a uranium mine and that he would sell them for a dollar a share. The American bought. A few days later the Canadian called and said, "That stock I sold you is up to $5 a share now, and I can let you have another 500 shares." The American bought. A little later the Canadian called again and said, "You know, I've got some good news for you. That uranium stock that you have? The shares have now gone up to $10 a share and I can still let you have another thousand shares."

"In that case," replied the American, "I will sell."

After a long pause, the Canadian on the other end of the line remarked, "WHO TO?"

* * * * * * * * * *

STREAKING

Faster than any of the new jet planes is the nudist who just spilled coffee on his lap.

****

Streaking is an epidemic of the epidermis.

****

A beautiful girl was streaking through the lobby of a plush hotel and was being pursued by an Army officer who was, to put it bluntly, nude. At the court martial, the lawyer won an acquittal by virtue of the following paragraph in the Army Code of Law Manual: "It is not compulsory for an officer to wear a uniform at all times, as long as he is suitably garbed for the sport in which he is engaged."

****

SUCCESS

If at first you do succeed, hide your astonishment.

****

It's thinking about the load that makes one tired.

****

The turtle never makes progress until he sticks out his neck.

****

The three most difficult things to do are to kiss your wife when she's leaning away from you; cross a fence when it's leaning toward you; and to alibi for something that you did wrong.

****

Men do not stumble over mountains, only molehills.

****

People can be divided into three groups—those who make things happen, those who watch things happen, and those who wonder what happened.

****

Nothing is impossible for the man who doesn't have to do it himself.

****

Dr. Arnold Lowe's formula: Do more than you need to do, learn more than you need to know, and be all that you can be.

****

Successful man—one who makes more money than his wife can spend. Successful woman—a woman who finds such a man.

****

Henry Ford said, "Coming together is a beginning; keeping together is progress; working together is success."

****

How on earth were the Israelis so successful in winning the six-day war? They had to be, they were renting their equipment from Hertz.

****

If at first you don't succeed, try again. And then if you don't succeed, give up. Why make a darned fool out of yourself.

****

Henry Ford said, "The harder I worked, the luckier I got."

****

To see the horizon one must look up.

****

A formula for success—think of a product that costs a dime, sells for a dollar, and is habit-forming.

****

Success comes by doing successfully one thing at a time.

****

Behind every man
Who's achieved success
Stands a good wife
And the IRS.

****

TAXES

Three commonly told lies: I put it in the mail yesterday. You'll feel better tomorrow. I'm from the IRS and I'm here to help you.

****

Said the IRS agent to the tax payer, "Your audit will be canceled if you can come up with an excuse that I have not heard before."

****

"You have a nice home," said a stranger to the landowner. "I imagine it will be worth about $80,000."

"Oh, no," replied the owner, "it's worth at least $125,000. Are you thinking about buying the home?"

"No," said the stranger, "I'm your local tax assessor."

* * * * * * * * * *

The reason people have so many accountants doing their returns is that it saves them time—sometimes up to 20 years.

* * * * * * * * * *

"I'm not in love with the present
For the good old days I pine
When the government lived within its income
And without so much of mine."

* * * * * * * * * *

You can criticize the president
You can criticize the vice president
You can criticize the Congress
But you have to hand it to the IRS.

* * * * * * * * * *

Our peak earning years coincide with IRS's peak taking years.

* * * * * * * * * *

Income tax time is when you feel bled, white and blue.

* * * * * * * * * *

If you don't know the price of success, the IRS will gladly furnish you a tax table.

* * * * * * * * * *

The bathtub was invented in 1850, and the telephone in 1875. You could have sat in the tub for 25 years without being interrupted by a ringing telephone.

* * * * * * * * * *

The telephone rang at 3 a.m. "Are you awake?" inquired the caller.

"Yeah, I had to get up to answer the phone anyway."

* * * * * * * * * *

At 2 a.m. a man called his neighbor and asked him to quiet his barking dog. The next night at 3 a.m. the neighbor returned the call stating that he had no dog.

* * * * * * * * * *

TEXAS

A man in New Jersey discovered a use for frogskins, so he advertised in the Wall Street Journal. A gentleman from Texas replied to the ad and stated that he could supply all the frogskins desired. The man from New Jersey put in an order for two dozen frogskins. He waited and waited for the supply to arrive. Finally a small package arrived in the mail. When he opened it up there was one lone frogskin with a note attached to it: "The noise fooled me."

* * * * * * * * * *

A Texan visiting Australia was telling that it took big saws to cut some of their homegrown watermelons. As they were visiting, a kangaroo bounced by, and the Texan inquired of the Australian what the animal was. The Australian said, "That's not an animal, that's a grasshopper."

****

Everything is big in Texas including their dust storms. One day while driving in Texas a visitor noticed a cowboy hat in the ditch. He ran down and scraped the sand off the hat, got past the brim, kept going and pretty soon discovered the hat was being worn by someone who had become totally imbedded in the sand. As he got below the eyebrows, below the nose, and below the mouth, the man said, "Go back to the car and get a shovel. I'm on horseback."

****

Here is to Texas and all other out-lying states.

****

Then there was the Texan that couldn't decide whether Texas has the world's largest or smallest midgets.

****

If all the ice glaciers in Alaska should melt, Texas would become one of our smallest states.

****

TRAVEL AND TOURISM

My wife loves to travel. I carry a picture of her wherever I go.

****

The airline stewardess asked the Reverend passenger if he'd like a drink. "No," he replied. "I'm too close to the main office."

183

****

The ship was sinking and the captain called all hands on deck. "Who among you can pray?"

"I can," replied the ensign.

"Then pray, shipmate," ordered the Captain. "The rest of you, put on your life jackets. We're one short."

****

I arrived here by plane this afternoon. When I got off the airplane I got a tremendous ovation. Seems that I loosened the wrong belt.

****

An elderly man went to the airline ticket counter and asked for a round trip ticket. The clerk asked, "Where to?" He said, "It doesn't make any difference 'cause I'm coming back here anyway."

****

I spent a lot of time and money one winter getting a suntan in Florida and when I got the hotel bill I turned white.

****

An elderly airline passenger was asked by the stewardess to fasten his safety belt. He said, "My dear young lady, I don't have to, I wore suspenders."

****

I just came back from a pleasure trip. I took my mother-in-law to the airport.

****

I took a cruise to the Canary Islands and never saw a canary. Then I went to the Virgin Islands and never saw a virgin.

****

When an airplane crashes the black box does not break. Why not make the entire plane of the black box material?

* * * * * * * * * *

On airplanes they have floating devices under your seat. Why not have a parachute—especially when the plane is flying over land?

* * * * * * * * * *

The level of pleasure
is more intense,
when you travel
at someone else's expense.

—Ruth Boorstin

* * * * * * * * * *

Florida has two main industries, tourists and alligators, and they skin them both.

* * * * * * * * * *

No one should ever ask where a person is from. If he is from South Dakota, he will tell you. If not, it will embarrass him.

* * * * * * * * * *

The most lonesome feeling I ever had was going the wrong way on a one-way street. The cop stopped me and asked me where I was going. I told him wherever it was I must be late because everyone else was already coming back.

* * * * * * * * * *

Travel broadens one—so does sitting at home in an easy chair.

* * * * * * * * * *

Short visits make for long friends.

* * * * * * * * * *

A gentleman was sitting in a bar reading an advertisement in the local Want Ad section which read, "Would like to have person to accompany me on trip to Florida."

After several drinks, he left the bar and drove up to the address given in the ad. He knocked on the door. The man came to the door and asked what the caller wanted.

"I came in response to your ad. I just wanted to tell you that I can't go."

* * * * * * * * * *

UNCLASSIFIED AND CENSORED

A wife had been nagging her sixty-five year old husband to go to the Social Security office to apply for Social Security. He finally made the trip and was gone just a short while. When he came back his wife inquired, "Gee, that didn't take long. What did you do?" He said, "I simply opened my shirt and showed them the grey hair on my chest and they knew I was age qualified." Then his wife replied, "What didn't you drop your pants? You probably would have gotten total disability."

* * * * * * * * * *

I have often wondered how a self-addressed envelope does it.

* * * * * * * * * *

Looking at your face I'm wondering if anyone else got hurt in the accident.

—Rickles

* * * * * * * * * *

186

"Your fly is open," said his wife. "Yes, I know dear. I'm doing an experiment. Yesterday I kept three buttons open on my shirt and my neck got stiff."

****

This trend will continue until it ends.

****

I spent two weeks one day in Moscow.

****

Censored section: They asked Ole Olson whether he served in World War II. "Yes," he replied, "on December 7, 1941, I attacked Pearl Olson."

****

Where is the Texas border? In bed with Suzie.

****

I had a dog named Rover but I renamed him Herpes because he wouldn't heal.

****

What is an innuendo? An ethnic suppository.

****

How do you know when a joke has a father?
When the punch line becomes apparent.

****

White man always lives
Between worry and doubt
He builds houses with windows to let light in
Then he puts up curtains to shut light out.

****

Why do Catholic cab drivers have their St. Christopher's on their dash? It's their Oscar for running over Masons.

****

It's okay to kiss a nun as long as you don't get into the habit.

****

He must be getting old, I see him putting prunes into his martinis.

****

Keeping up with the Jones'
Is getting me down.
Can't keep up
with Smith or Brown.

****

A politician was asked his position on Bosnia. He said, "I don't really know, but my wife likes it."

****

"Bam, Bam, Bee
Kick 'em in the knee
Bam, Bam, Bass
Kick 'em in the other knee."

—Jerry Lewis

****

A Catholic married a Protestant but was able to convert her to the Catholic faith. After she died, he again married a Protestant and again was able to convert his second wife into the Catholic faith. When she also died and at his third marriage he was not successful in getting his wife to change religious affiliations, so the Father approached him one day and said, "Say, Herb, how come you've not been able to bring your new wife into the church?"

"Well Father," he said, "the old converter is not what he used to be."

****

How are rain and sex similar? You always think your neighbor gets more than you do.

****

Love has many pains, but celibacy has no pleasures.

****

An Indian went to see the doctor and said, "My problem is I can't sleep." The doctor gave him some sleeping pills and told him to come back the next week to see how he was doing. He came back the next week and reported he still couldn't sleep, not even to get a nap. The doctor said he would give him some different pills. The Indian said that there was a whole bunch of Indians at the reservation who couldn't sleep. The doctor said, "How many of them are there?" The Indian answered, "About 500." The doctor said, "Is that so? What do you call your Tribe?" Replied the Indian, "We call ourselves 'Indian Napless 500'."

****

Virgin Wool comes from fast running female sheep.

****

Said the father to his son, "I can see right through that girl's intrigue."
"Yes, father I know but that's the way they all dress nowadays."

****

So you want to start a movement — eat a prune.

****

Did you hear about the fellow that was so narrow minded that he could look through a keyhole with both eyes.

****

The last time my friend had a cough like that it nearly killed him — he was in his neighbor's closet.

* * * * * * * * * *

I never repeat gossip, so listen carefully the first time.

* * * * * * * * * *

The good thing about modern art is that it's not as bad as it is painted.

* * * * * * * * * *

"No, Lulu, an alabaster isn't an illegitimate Mohammedan."

* * * * * * * * * *

This is my first visit to your blighted area.

* * * * * * * * * *

"May I present my wife?"
"No, thanks, I already have one."

* * * * * * * * * *

Said one strawberry to another: "If I had not been planted in the same bed with you, we wouldn't be in this jam together."

* * * * * * * * * *

The bunny girls at the Playboy Clubs are on strike. They want more lettuce.

* * * * * * * * * *

Halitosis is better than no breath at all.

* * * * * * * * * *

Her breath takes her beauty away.

* * * * * * * * * *

I never met a man I didn't like. I forget now whether it was Will Rogers or Elizabeth Taylor that said that.

* * * * * * * * * *

I'm real good to my wife, I never go home.

****

Did you hear what happened to the girl with the cotton stockings?
Nothing.

****

Nonchalance: The ability to look like an owl when you've behaved like an ass.

****

Don't put off until tomorrow what you can do today. If you enjoy it, you can do it again tomorrow — if you're young enough.

****

I was kidding one of my good friends the other day and he told me, "Al, you can go straight to hell." I quickly replied, "George, that's the first time I've ever had an invitation to your home."

****

Here's to Adam,
Father of us all,
He was Johnny on the spot,
When the leaves began to fall.

****

If a cluttered desk is indicative of a cluttered mind, is an empty desk indicative of an empty mind?

****

I think my husband would make a good member of the Ku Klux Klan — he's such a devil under the sheet.

****

A girl's plans for the future seldom take shape before she does.

* * * * * * * * * *

He: "I'd kiss you, but I have scruples."
She: "Oh, that's OK. I've been vaccinated for that."

* * * * * * * * * *

Many a woman has started out playing with fire and ended up cooking over it.

* * * * * * * * * *

A gossip is a person with a keen sense of rumor.

* * * * * * * * * *

The habits of rabbits
Are such it's agreed
That dozens of cousins
Are common indeed.

* * * * * * * * * *

A new hotel in Las Vegas caters exclusively to about-to-be-divorcees. It's called the Jiltin-Hilton.

* * * * * * * * * *

Smile — it adds to your face value.

* * * * * * * * * *

Keep smiling. It makes people wonder what you've been up to.

* * * * * * * * * *

UNDERTAKER

A cadaver lying on the table was being prepared for burial by two funeral directors. The one noticed that the cadaver had a winning lottery ticket in his pocket. The other replied, "The lucky stiff."

—Gary Larsen from The Far Side

* * * * * * * * * *

You'll have a bad day if you walk into an antique store and ask what's new or into a crematory and asked what's cooking.

* * * * * * * * * *

In spite of all the enormous advances in medical science, funeral directors seem to be unworried.

* * * * * * * * * *

Did you hear about the undertaker who took a PR course in how to look sad at a $3,000 funeral.

* * * * * * * * * *

An undertaker is the type of person that will let you down in the end.

* * * * * * * * * *

Down South they call an undertaker a Southern planter.

* * * * * * * * * *

An undertaker's business is always going into the hole.

* * * * * * * * * *

Undertaking is primarily an ushering out profession.

* * * * * * * * * *

Did we ever have a big rain yesterday! The rain gauge you set in my garden measured eight inches yesterday morning. It was a bit yellowish. Darn that dog!

****

Was it ever cold. You bet! The other day my secretary came to work wearing turtle-necked panty hose.

****

Yes, it was cold last winter. It took me almost two days to dislodge my dog from the fire hydrant.

****

Noah asked his wife, "Why do you always have to say that into each life some rain must fall?"

****

"So you're from Dakota? The weather must be terrible."
"Oh no! We have four seasons: early winter, mid-winter, late winter and next winter."

****

Was it dry during the thirties? You bet! I'll give you a few examples. Cows were so thin that you could brand calves two at a time using carbon paper. Hogs were so thin that when you sent them to Morrells, they could make bacon with rinds on both sides. The grass was so brown and burnt that the only way to get cows to eat it was to put green goggles on them. The grass was only about one inch high, the grasshoppers had to lay on their backs to eat it.

****

I'm waiting for spring and I won't take snow for an answer.

****

Do you get a lot of snow in South Dakota? No, but a lot goes through there.

****

The other day it was so cold that I saw a chicken cross the street with it's capon.

****

"It was so cold," said my friend from North Dakota, "that it would freeze the ears off a brass monkey."

****

On a hot summer day, Pat asked his friend Mike how his wife was standing the heat. Mike replied, "Pat, I really don't know, she's been dead for only a week you know."

****

A fellow stayed up all night wondering when the sun would come up and the next morning it dawned on him.

****

It was so hot in South Dakota in 1936 that I saw a dog chasing a cat and they were both walking.

****

South Dakota is caught in the deep-freeze,
We walk around numb,
Way up to our knees,
We quiver and shake,
Like a mighty earthquake,
And blow icicles when we sneeze.

****

During the severe drought of the 30's, a rain drop fell on the head of an Oklahoman. They had to throw two buckets of sand on his face to revive him.

****

In our section of the country we always get two rains—
one too early and one too late.

* * * * * * * * * *

This unusual weather is more unusual than usual.

* * * * * * * * * *

It was so cold the other morning that when I set out a
pan of boiling water it froze so fast that the ice was still
warm.

* * * * * * * * * *

It's been so dry lately that the rain that we did get had
only 40% moisture.

* * * * * * * * * *

He holds so many degrees that his friends call him Mr.
Fahrenheit.

* * * * * * * * * *

It was so dry that trees chased dogs.

* * * * * * * * * *

Our drought was so bad that during the time of Noah's
flood, we got only 2 1/2 inches of rain in our section of the
country.

* * * * * * * * * *

An old timer was reminiscing about the severe drought
of the 30's. "Why, even the earth got big cracks in it. One
noon I accidentally dropped a wrench into a crack on my
way to lunch, and when I got back, I could still hear it drop-
ping."

* * * * * * * * * *

What's so wonderful about living where it gets to 30
degrees below zero in the wintertime? Well, the big attrac-
tion is that there are no mosquitoes.

****

My farm is located too far north for the south rains, and too far south for the north rains.

****

WOMEN

She's a real beauty. Her eyes pick-pocket my heart.

****

I'd like to introduce my wife
to others as my daughter
It pleases her and takes the place
of gifts I might have bought her.

****

I've often wondered why women worry about equality when they are already superior.

****

If women dressed to please men they would dress a lot faster.

****

"Do you like my hat?" she asked. "Yes," remarked her husband. "And do wear it regardless of what people say."

****

Here's a toast to women and all other expenses.

****

I love women for a good reason. Half my ancestors were women.

****

197

She was a wonderful housekeeper. After every divorce she kept the house.

* * * * * * * * * *

Is my wife ever frugal! She even sends Kleenex to the laundry.

* * * * * * * * * *

God created man, rested for a few days took a look and said to himself, "I can do better," so he created woman. Since that time no one has rested.

* * * * * * * * * *

Judging by the time it takes some ladies to fix themselves up, one can note that a thing of beauty is a job forever.

* * * * * * * * * *

I like to give my wife a lot of credit, but she usually insists on cash.

* * * * * * * * * *

Husband: "My wife does bird imitations."
Friend: "For instance?"
Husband: "She watches me like a hawk."

* * * * * * * * * *

Roseanne Barr is the kind of gal you'd like to return to her mother.

* * * * * * * * * *

The clerk said to the lady, "This hat will make you look ten years younger."
"Then I don't want it," replied the lady, "because when I take it off it will make me look ten years older."

* * * * * * * * * *

He called his wife casserole because she is a dish that has everything.

* * * * * * * * *

Every five seconds in the United States a woman gives birth to a new baby — we must find that woman.

* * * * * * * * *

Women started the liberation movement because they were tired of dancing backwards. And now when they go to the filling station they say, "Fill him up."

* * * * * * * * *

Women are remarkable creatures whereas men can't say much.

* * * * * * * * *

She sends me out with my conscience while she sits at home flirting with her imagination.

* * * * * * * * *

I guess my wife quit smoking cigarettes. I found cigar butts in the ashtray.

* * * * * * * * *

My wife went through three red lights the other day — two of them were on the back of a truck.

* * * * * * * * *

When a woman sticks her hand out of a car window it means that the window is down.

* * * * * * * * *

When man was first introduced to woman, Adam went up to Eve and said, "Madam, I'm Adam."

* * * * * * * * *

Eve asked Adam, "Do you still love me?" And Adam replied, "Who else?"

* * * * * * * * *

The Russians have discovered something that will do the work of ten men — namely, ten women.

* * * * * * * * *

WORK

A Texan was playing poker which included an Englishman. The Englishman drew four aces and then said, "I will bet a pound." Said the Texan, "Don't you Englishmen know how to count? I'm going to raise you a ton."

* * * * * * * * *

Memo on the employees bulletin board: If you haven't developed a hernia, you're not carrying your share of the load.

* * * * * * * * *

Once there were two boll weevils. One worked hard and became a big shot; the other, the lesser of two weevils.

* * * * * * * * *

The son said to his father, "Yes, I know that hard work never killed anyone, but I'd sure hate to be it's first victim."

* * * * * * * * *

A letter of recommendation: To whom it may concern. This person worked less than three weeks and we are satisfied.

* * * * * * * * *

The reason worry kills more people than work is that more people worry than work.

****

If you watch the clock, you will always be one of the hands.

****

Your salary increase will be effective as soon as you are.

****

Being wrong is one of the things that I do best, and I'm getting better at it.

****

God made the world, but the Dutch made Holland.

****

The only thing worse than work is looking for work.

****

It is better to put 10 men to work than to do the work of ten men.

****

Work is one of God's greatest gifts.

****

Work ethic: Once our people were busy as beavers, now they are as playful as otters.

****

"I'm puzzled," said the doctor, "you seem to be suffering from overwork, but nobody does that any more."

****

I'm for it.

* * * * * * * * * *

Barefoot boy with cheek of tan,
Are you a boy, my little man?
Or are you, with your hair aswirl,
No boy at all? Are you a girl?
And in those faded jeans with patches
And shirt so tattered (nothing matches),
Are you a starveling, lacking care?
Or offspring of a millionaire?

—Richard Armour

* * * * * * * * * *

WILSHIRE SELF-IMPROVEMENT LIBRARY

HUMOR

SELF-HELP & INSPIRATIONAL

Available from your bookstore or directly from Wilshire Book Company.
Please add $2.00 shipping and handling for each book ordered.

Wilshire Book Company

12015 Sherman Road
No. Hollywood, California 91605
For our complete catalog, visit our Web site at http://www.mpowers.com.

NEW. . . by Marcia Grad

Author of *Charisma: How to get that "special magic"*

THE PRINCESS WHO BELIEVED
IN
FAIRY TALES

"Here is a very special book that will guide you lovingly into a new way of thinking about yourself and your life so that the future will be filled with hope and love and song."

OG MANDINO
Author, *The Greatest Salesman in the World*

The Princess Who Believed in Fairy Tales is a personal growth book of the rarest kind. It is a delightful, humor-filled story you will experience so deeply that it can literally change your feelings about yourself, your relationships, and your life.

The princess' journey of self-discovery on the Path of Truth is an eye-opening, inspiring, empowering psychological and spiritual journey that symbolizes the one we all take through life as we sort out illusion from reality, come to terms with our childhood dreams and pain, and discover who we really are and how life works.

If you have struggled with childhood pain, with feelings of not being good enough, with the loss of your dreams, or if you have been disappointed in your relationships, *The Princess Who Believed in Fairy Tales* will prove to you that happy endings—and new beginnings—are always possible. Or if you simply want to get closer to your own truth, the princess will guide you.

You will experience the princess' journey as your own. You will laugh with her and cry with her, learn with her and grow with her, and if you are in pain, you will begin to heal with her.

The universal appeal to both men and women of *The Princess Who Believed in Fairy Tales* has resulted in its translation into numerous languages.

<u>Excerpts from Readers' Heartfelt Letters</u>

"*The Princess* is truly a gem! Though I've read a zillion self-help and spiritual books, I got more out of this one than from any other one I've ever read. It is just too illuminating and full of wisdom to ever be able to thank you enough."

"Your loving story tells my story and many other women's so beautifully. I related to each page for different reasons. Thank you for putting my experience into words for me. . . . I've been waiting to read this book my entire life."

Available at bookstores. Or send $10.00 (CA res. $10.83) plus $2.00 S/H to Wilshire Book Company, 12015 Sherman Road, No. Hollywood, CA 91605.

For our complete catalog, visit our Web site at www.mpowers.com.

A Personal Invitation from the Publisher, Melvin Powers...

There is a wonderful, unique book titled *The Knight in Rusty Armor* that is guaranteed to captivate your imagination as you discover the secret of what is most important in life. It is a delightful tale of a desperate knight in search of his true self.

Since we first published *The Knight in Rusty Armor,* we have received an unprecedented number of calls and letters from readers praising its powerful insights and entertaining style. It is a memorable, fun-filled story, rich in wit and humor, that has changed thousands of lives for the better. *The Knight* is one of our most popular titles. It has been published in numerous languages and has become a well-known favorite in many countries. I feel so strongly about this book that personally extending an invitation for you to read it.

The Knight in Rusty Armor

Join the knight as he faces a life-changing dilemma upon discovering that he is trapped in his armor, just as *we* may be trapped in *our* armor—an invisible kind that we use to protect ourselves from others and from various aspects of life.

As the knight searches for a way to free himself, he receives guidance from the wise sage Merlin the Magician, who encourages him to embark on the most difficult crusade of his life. The knight takes up the challenge and travels the Path of Truth, where he meets his real self for the first time and confronts the Universal Truths that govern his life—and ours.

The knight's journey reflects our own, filled with hope and despair, belief and disillusionment, laughter and tears. His insights become our insights as we follow along on his intriguing adventure of self-discovery. Anyone who has ever struggled with the meaning of life and love will discover profound wisdom and truth as this unique fantasy unfolds. *The Knight in Rusty Armor* is an experience that will expand your mind, touch your heart, and nourish your soul.

Available at all bookstores. Or send $5.00 (CA res. $5.41) plus $2.00 S/H to Wilshire Book Company, 12015 Sherman Road, No. Hollywood, CA 91605.

For our complete catalog, visit our Web site at www.mpowers.com.

Books by Melvin Powers

HOW TO GET RICH IN MAIL ORDER

1. How to Develop Your Mail Order Expertise 2. How to Find a Unique Product or Service to Sell 3. How to Make Money with Classified Ads 4. How to Make Money with Display Ads 5. The Unlimited Potential for Making Money with Direct Mail 6. How to Copycat Successful Mail Order Operations 7. How I Created a Bestseller Using the Copycat Technique 8. How to Start and Run a Profitable Mail Order Special Interest Book Business 9. I Enjoy Selling Books by Mail—Some of My Successful Ads 10. Five of My Most Successful Direct Mail Pieces That Sold and Are Selling Millions of Dollars' Worth of Books 11. Melvin Powers's Mail Order Success Strategy—Follow it and You'll Become a Millionaire 12. How to Sell Your Products to Mail Order Companies, Retail Outlets, Jobbers, and Fund Raisers for Maximum Distribution and Profit 13. How to Get Free Display Ads and Publicity that Will Put You on the Road to Riches 14. How to Make Your Advertising Copy Sizzle 15. Questions and Answers to Help You Get Started Making Money 16. A Personal Word from Melvin Powers 17. How to Get Started 18. Selling Products on Television   8½" x 11½" — 352 Pages . . . $20.00

MAKING MONEY WITH CLASSIFIED ADS

1. Getting Started with Classified Ads 2. Everyone Loves to Read Classified Ads 3. How to Find a Money-Making Product 4. How to Write Classified Ads that Make Money 5. What I've Learned from Running Thousands of Classified Ads 6. Classified Ads Can Help You Make Big Money in Multi-Level Programs 7. Two-Step Classified Ads Made Me a Multi-Millionaire—They Can Do the Same for You! 8. One-Inch Display Ads Can Work Wonders 9. Display Ads Can Make You a Fortune Overnight 10. Although I Live in California, I Buy My Grapefruit from Florida 11. Nuts and Bolts of Mail Order Success 12. What if You Can't Get Your Business Running Successfully? What's Wrong? How to Correct it 13. Strategy for Mail Order Success   8½" x 11½" — 240 Pages . . . $20.00

HOW TO SELF-PUBLISH YOUR BOOK AND HAVE THE FUN AND EXCITEMENT OF BEING A BEST-SELLING AUTHOR

1. Who is Melvin Powers? 2. What is the Motivation Behind Your Decision to Publish Your Book? 3. Why You Should Read This Chapter Even if You Already Have an Idea for a Book 4. How to Test the Salability of Your Book Before You Write One Word 5. How I Achieved Sales Totaling $2,000,000 on My Book *How to Get Rich in Mail Order* 6. How to Develop a Second Career by Using Your Expertise 7. How to Choose an Enticing Book Title 8. Marketing Strategy 9. Success Stories 10. How to Copyright Your Book 11. How to Write a Winning Advertisement 12. Advertising that Money Can't Buy 13. Questions and Answers to Help You Get Started 14. Self-Publishing and the Midas Touch
          8½" x 11½" — 240 Pages . . . $20.00

A PRACTICAL GUIDE TO SELF-HYPNOSIS

1. What You Should Know about Self-Hypnosis 2. What about the Dangers of Hypnosis? 3. Is Hypnosis the Answer? 4. How Does Self-Hypnosis Work? 5. How to Arouse Yourself From the Self-Hypnotic State 6. How to Attain Self-Hypnosis 7. Deepening the Self-Hypnotic State 8. What You Should Know about Becoming an Excellent Subject 9. Techniques for Reaching the Somnambulistic State 10. A New Approach to Self-Hypnosis 11. Psychological Aids and Their Function 12. Practical Applications of Self-Hypnosis
          144 Pages . . . $10.00

Available at your bookstore or directly from Wilshire Book Company.
Please add $2.00 shipping and handling for each book ordered.

Wilshire Book Company
12015 Sherman Road, No. Hollywood, California 91605

For our complete catalog, visit our Web site at http://www.mpowers.com.